D1408089

Navigating Midlife

Navigating Midlife

Using Typology as a Guide

Eleanor S. Corlett
Nancy B. Millner

Davies-Black Publishing
Palo Alto, California

For John and B

Published by Davies-Black Publishing, an imprint of Consulting Psychologists Press, Inc., 3803 East Bayshore Road, Palo Alto, CA 94303; 800-624-1765.

Special discounts on bulk quantities of Davies-Black Publishing books are available to corporations, professional associations, and other organizations. For details, contact the Director of Book Sales at Davies-Black Publishing, 3803 East Bayshore Road, Palo Alto, California 94303; 650-691-9123; Fax 650-988-0673.

Copyright © 1993 by Eleanor S. Corlett and Nancy B. Millner. All rights reserved. No part of this book may be reproduced, stored in a retrieval system, or transmitted in any form or by any means, electronic, mechanical, photocopying, recording, or otherwise, without written permission of the publisher.

Myers-Briggs Type Indicator and MBTI are registered trademarks of Consulting Psychologists Press, Inc.

The following publishers have generously given permission to use extended quotations from copyrighted works: From *Necessary Losses*, by Judith Viorst. Copyright 1986 by Judith Viorst. Reprinted by permission of Simon & Schuster, Inc. From *Seven Arrows*, by Hyemeyosts Storm. Copyright 1972 by Hyemeyosts Storm. Reprinted by permission of HarperCollins Publishers. From *Memories, Dreams and Reflections*, by C. G. Jung. Reprinted by permission of Random House, Inc. From *The Undiscovered Self*, by C. G. Jung. Reprinted by permission of Little, Brown and Company. From *The Well and the Cathedral*, by Ira Progoff. Copyright 1977 by Dialogue House. Reprinted by permission of Dialogue House. From *Man and His Symbols*, by C. G. Jung. Copyright 1964 by Anchor Press. Reprinted by permission of Anchor Press. From *In Midlife: A Jungian Perspective*, by Murray Stein. Reprinted by permission of Spring Publications.

Printed in the United States of America
02 01 00 99 98   15 14 13 12 11 10 9 8 7 6

Library of Congress Cataloging-in-Publication Data
Corlett, Eleanor
    Navigating midlife : using typology as a guide / Eleanor Corlett,
Nancy Millner.
       p.   cm.
    Includes bibliographical references and index.
    ISBN 0-89106-061-8
    1. Middle age--Psychological aspects. 2. Middle aged persons--Psychology.
3. Typology (Psychology) 4. Jung, C. G. (Carl Gustav), 1875-1961.
I. Millner, Nancy, 1939- . II. Title.
BF724.6.C67   1993
155.6'6—dc20

                                                        93-4374
                                                         CIP

First printing 1993

Contents

Contents

Part 3 Further Explorations on Type

Foreword

I say with Didacus Stella [that] a dwarf
standing on the shoulders of a giant may see farther
than a giant himself.

Robert Burton (1577–1640)

Carl G. Jung was a giant in the history of ideas. His work changed our perspective of the world and ourselves. However, the continued vitality and usefulness of the ideas of a giant rest on those who follow and enable us to continually see farther and farther.

Navigating Midlife: Using Typology as a Guide is a book that enables us to see farther. It is a practical how-to book illuminating the midlife experience through the perspective of Jungian psychological type theory and the *Myers-Briggs Type Indicator®* (MBTI®). Isabel Briggs Myers and Katharine Cook Briggs' development of the MBTI, a personality inventory that gives people access to their personality type, was a major advancement in the application of Jungian ideas. The genius of Myers' contribution is that she was able to take one piece of her knowledge of complex Jungian theory, the theory of psychological type, and make it understandable and useful to a vast number of people.

This accomplishment opened the door to "the psychology that works." As the MBTI moved into wider use, the initial focus of interpretation has been on learning one's type, with its potential gifts and pitfalls, and on recognizing and appreciating individual differences. This focus pro-vided a powerful tool for helping people understand themselves and others, and with this focus a phenomenal growth took place in the MBTI's application in education, counseling, and management. A major task for the creative leaders of the generation who have followed Isabel Myers is to lead people who are interested in type theory and individual differences toward a deeper understanding and use of Jungian theory—to move beyond an introductory interpretation of psychological type through type dynamics and type development to the model of the psyche and the process of individuation, the ultimate goal of individual development.

Eleanor Corlett and Nancy Millner have provided a resource that leads us step by step into the richness of this expanded territory. They have delineated the connection between psychological type theory and the Jungian model of personality and human development and have provided an enriched framework for understanding the midlife journey. In documenting the way that psychological type actually plays out in individual people's lives as they travel through an often puzzling and ill-understood stage of life, they both confirm and expand Jungian ideas about human development and the path toward individuation. In returning to a mandala formulation of type development, Corlett and Millner provide a renewed flexibility to the current linear model. All of this provides a powerful foundation for an in-depth application of the Jungian perspective to daily living and conscious growth throughout the life span, as well as to the midlife experience.

The exploration that led to this book was a journey I shared with Eleanor Corlett and Nancy Millner through the beginning terrain. It was a happy and fulfilling collaboration. The bulk of the journey and the difficult terrain was theirs. The creativity, intelligence, and diligence they brought to the task has produced a book that exceeds our original vision.

This book will be invaluable to all those in midlife, to those who are in professional, personal, or helping relationships with people experiencing midlife, and to all those desiring to move past an introductory knowledge of psychological type to the full richness of Jungian personality theory. It is an important contribution to the life of Jungian theory and the MBTI, but also to personal growth and development.

Katharine D. Myers

Preface

We have written this book in the belief that midlife is an important developmental life stage and that the theory of psychological type as conceptualized by C. G. Jung and measured by the *Myers-Briggs Type Indicator®* (MBTI®) personality inventory*, along with other dimensions of Jungian theory, can be helpful guides for viewing and navigating the transition successfully. Increasing one's understanding of midlife dynamics and one's own psychological type preferences can help lead to the successful resolution of issues that often arise at midlife, benefitting the individual experiencing the transition as well as society as a whole. This book is designed for those experiencing the dynamics of midlife—at whatever point in life they occur—and for those who are living or working with them as they undergo this transition. This book may also be helpful to people who wish to explore midlife in some depth by using the combined insights that Jungian psychology and psychological type provide.

We believe that Jung's conceptualizations of midlife transition, Murray Stein's midlife stage theory, and one's psychological type are effective

---

*The *Myers-Briggs Type Indicator* (MBTI) is an inventory based on Jungian psychological type theory that yields sixteen personality types.

tools—though certainly not the only tools—that individuals can use to explore their own personal midlife experience. While we do not suggest that an awareness of these models is a prerequisite for development, they are powerful and helpful tools for people who want to reflect consciously on the midlife process. Under the guidance of Katharine D. Myers, who designed and presented the first of the programs addressing midlife development and the MBTI personality inventory which we have since continued, we became familiar with the work of Jung and Stein on midlife. We then began to explore our own midlife journeys to determine in which ways they were or were not true to the theories of Jung and Stein. We found the theories to be generally true and helpful, but we also discovered that they did not always accurately reflect our own experiences. We then decided that we wanted to use Jung's and Stein's theories to explore both the differences and the similarities that we found. Our familiarity with the MBTI instrument left us very interested in discovering how people with different personality orientations—that is, different MBTI type codes—would experience and cope with a common life transition. We found that the people who shared their midlife experiences with us through workshops, classes, interviews, and questionnaires validated Jung's concepts of the midlife transition process in their own lives, as well as reflected many type-related differences in the way they experienced the transition.

We wanted to examine the different ways that people experienced midlife. Jung insisted that observable fact and experience were more relevant than theory. While we have found the experiences that others have shared with us to be valuable, we have also found the insights offered by Jung and others to be beneficial. We found a great richness in the experiences others shared with us and became increasingly interested in gaining a better understanding of their journeys. We wanted to understand their stories as they expressed them. We hoped that if we listened closely enough without preconceptions, we might gain fresh insight into the impact of psychological type on the midlife journey.

Furthermore, we wanted to explore additional dimensions of psychological type development theory as a part of Jung's broader theory of the individuation process, with the idea that doing so would help us move toward a more holistic view of psychological type development. We believe that if people who work primarily with typology can learn more about life stage development and Jung's individuation process (of which type development is a significant part), and if people who work primarily with other aspects of Jung's theories can see that psychological type theory provides a framework for individuation and a lens through which the psyche can be viewed, everyone can benefit.

We created this book for people who see the value of using a concrete instrument, namely, the MBTI personality inventory, to begin an in-depth study of personality development. Before discussing midlife development in the context that is described in this book, the MBTI personality inventory should be administered by a qualified professional and interpreted with individuals so that they can understand and confirm their type codes. A confirmed four-letter type code is necessary if the kind of exploration found in this book is to be most meaningful.

We believe that psychological type theory, when integrated into our personal and professional lives, can enhance and broaden our understanding of individual development, personal relationships, and group interaction. Yet we also understand that psychological type will not provide a complete answer to any human process or experience. A simple four-letter type code cannot explain the richness and complexity of any one person. Even as we concentrate our work on the use of the MBTI personality inventory as a tool for understanding midlife, we recognize the many other variables that need consideration.

Our primary objective is to share our insights about the midlife experience for each of the sixteen psychological types identified by the inventory. We do this by reporting on the work of Jung and others, and by sharing the experiences of people who represent the sixteen different psychological types. These people have largely reported their experiences in our type and midlife workshops over the past ten years throughout the United States. We have also collected questionnaire data, conducted interviews, and tracked counseling clients. Individually and together we have presented the concepts of psychological type, Jungian theory, and Stein's midlife stage theory. We then together, and in consultation with others, reviewed the data we collected, searching for consistent themes and psychological type patterns. Whenever our findings indicated expanded dimensions of psychological type, we then attempted to validate these findings with individuals and groups.

Patterns and questions then emerged. The patterns led us to agree with those who espouse that there are many paths of type development and also to suggest that the midlife experience may be most successfully explored through a holistic, mandala model for understanding type theory and the individuation process. We will present this approach in detail in this book.

The profiles in this book are composites based primarily on the behaviors or observations of many people who share the same or similar type preferences. The patterns are true, yet these profiles should not necessarily be considered true for every person of that type. They are representations reflecting true patterns, yet are incomplete pictures of any one individual.

We begin this book by exploring some general themes of midlife and looking at their possible meanings. We then explore midlife within the larger context of human development and examine the stages of midlife transition, emphasizing how people with different psychological types experience their transition.

Finally, we offer this book with the hope that by attempting to honor both the life experiences that people have shared with us and our expanding knowledge of Jungian thought, we can make a contribution to the understanding of midlife and psychological type theory.

Part 1

Midlife: A Survey of the Territory

Chapter 1

Glimpses of Midlife

*We had the experience
but missed the meaning.*

T. S. Eliot

In many ways, the midlife transition is like any other transition people pass through in life involving lifestyle changes, careers, relationships, and all the joys and difficulties of being human. Yet it is also about much more. Successful midlife transition has at its core elements that distinguish it from all other life transitions—the search for one's authentic self and one's unique mission and purpose.

At midlife people often feel split, finding themselves concerned with matters of everyday, practical importance on the one hand, and with matters of meaning and purpose on the other. People experiencing midlife often ask themselves not only *how* they are to live but *why*, a question that points to the very meaning of their lives.

Midlife transition, which typically occurs near the middle of life, is about matters of spirit, mission, and culture. Spirit refers to the need to feel connected to something greater than oneself, mission refers to one's purpose in life, and culture refers to the society left for future generations. The transition is also about the ordinary concerns of everyday life and self-development in the realm of such matters as coping with physical aging, teenage children, aging parents, and job pressures.

We will first plot the terrain of the midlife journey by looking at the typical experiences of this period and suggesting their possible meanings. Next, we will introduce readers to the ideas of Jungian typology as a tool for understanding our perceptions as we move at midlife from fitting into our environment toward becoming our own unique selves. We will then place midlife in the larger context of human development and move from the general themes of midlife to its various stages, considering how Jungian psychology and psychological type theory can illuminate our understanding. Special attention will then be devoted to the different ways that people with different psychological type preferences experience midlife. Finally, we will take a look at how spirituality, a significant dimension of the midlife experience, is addressed by people with different psychological type preferences. While all people in midlife transition may encounter similar themes common to midlife—clearly psychological type is not the only factor that influences the perception of the experience— looking at the experience with the benefit that a knowledge of type theory provides can nevertheless add another important dimension. By being aware of how type preferences influence the way people tend to cope with midlife, we can perhaps better understand our own midlife transitions as well as those of others.

Confusion, Ambiguity, and Frustration

Questions often mark the beginning of the midlife transition, though they are not always recognized or clearly articulated. One simply has the feeling that something is going on. Feelings of discontent, boredom, anxiety, or of an inability to concentrate are common. People report feeling that their lives are too restricted or small or that something is missing. Some feel excited and adventuresome; others feel that their lives are being torn from them, suffering losses outside their control.

Lurking under the surface, if not above it, are various questions such as:

- Who am I really?
- What do I want to do with the time I have left in my life?
- Have my previous choices been good choices?
- What will it cost me to make changes in my life?
- Will any changes I make be worth it?
- What is the meaning of all this?

During this period of ambiguity and confusion, people often feel they don't know their way. They don't know how long this part of the journey will last, and they don't know what the risks are or why they must travel through it. People simply know they must grow and go forward.

Tolstoy (James, 1961) beautifully expressed the dynamics of this period. At about the age of 50, Tolstoy began to experience moments of perplexity. He didn't know how he should live or what he should do. He was simply aware that his life had lost its meaning:

> I felt that something had broken within me on which my life had always rested, and that I had nothing left to hold on to, and that morally my life had stopped....It cannot be said exactly that I wished to kill myself, for the force which drew me away from life was fuller, more powerful, more general than any mere desire. It was a force like my old aspiration to live, only it impelled me in the opposite direction. It was an aspiration of my whole being to get out of life.
>
> All this took place at a time when so far as my outer circumstances went, I ought to have been completely happy. I had a good wife who loved me and whom I loved; good children and a large property which was increasing with no pains taken on my part. I was more respected by my kinsfolk and acquaintances than I had ever been; I was loaded with praise by strangers; and without exaggeration I could believe my name already famous. Moreover, I was neither insane nor ill....And yet, I could give no reasonable meaning to any actions of my life. And I was surprised that I had not understood this from the very beginning. (p. 150–151)

Tolstoy asked himself hard questions. He wanted to know what the outcome of his potential accomplishments might be. He asked who he might be and what he might do tomorrow. He wondered why he should live and if there could be any purpose in life that death could not undo and destroy.

Tolstoy's experience is not unlike those of other people in midlife, who face similar questions, struggles, and quests for meaning. People often sense the ultimate importance of knowing who they are, but also find it impossible to know specifically what these things mean in the context of their everyday lives. This phenomenon often manifests itself as anxiety and as agonizing difficulty with decision making, as was the case with a single mother of two who was facing a painful midlife vocational choice. She described her midlife transition as feeling as though she were stuck in the center of a circle, perceiving that choices surrounded her, but that she couldn't move toward any one of them. She felt bombarded by a constantly agonizing, pushing, driving force:

> I slept with it every night and lived with it each day. It was not just wondering what I was going to do. It was that breathless, breathstopping, "God, what am I going to do? Please stop pushing me. Let me have peace; let me find safety. My fingers just can't hold on anymore." It was as if I lived in a continual emergency necessitating a decision which was just out of reach at that time.

For this woman and others, confusion, disharmony, and conflict are constant companions. The past and future seem disconnected. Safety and security pull one back toward the past, but it feels too small and too binding. Growth pulls one forward toward a different place, but it is out of focus, unknown, and frightening.

Loss and Gain

The recognition of loss is almost always required before one can move ahead at midlife. The confusion many experience during midlife stems

4

from a loss of assurance, security, and clarity; there are often other losses as well. During this time, some things die and others are born. Occasionally things are consciously left behind, as when people change roles, leave jobs and/or relationships, or alter lifestyles and friendships. Often losses are not voluntary but are instead imposed—sometimes with painful consequences. Death, divorce, job loss, a loss of youth and/or health, and other such losses are rarely chosen.

Feelings of powerlessness, dependency, and lack of self-worth often accompany such losses. One person describing his dismissal from a job he had had for twenty years said, "When I lost that job I just kept asking myself what I was going to do and what I could do to be worth something."

Jung (1965), who perhaps more than any other person has plotted the terrain of midlife transition, describes in his autobiography the loss of his academic career at midlife and the risk that it involved:

> I abandoned my academic career. For I felt that something great was happening to me, and I put my trust in the thing....I knew that it would fill my life and for the sake of that goal I was ready to take any kind of risk. (p. 194)

Loss is painful, yet it can offer opportunity for growth and new understandings.

Risk and Fear of Change

Risk and the fear of it are ever present during times of change. We found that change seemed more difficult for some people than others and that individual differences influence the way people make changes and how quickly they implement them. To resist change is almost certain to bring about some kind of negative result, as the story below illustrates.

A highly respected and effective manager of a large law firm understood rigidity well, remembering his father, whom he did not wish to emulate:

My father stopped his life at about 35 or 40. He simply set his jaw, gritted his teeth, and stood firm against a changing world. During the last twenty years of his life, you could see his jaw setting more and more rigidly. He died of a heart attack at 63.

But the problem is not always that people resist change. Some people are too eager to change. They respond reactively before undergoing the difficult, inner, time-consuming exploration necessary to determine the kind of change appropriate for them. Their task is to learn a measured approach. Change must be handled carefully and must be addressed consciously.

Inner Focus

Choices must be made during the midlife transition, just as they must be made during any transition in life. However, the key characteristic of midlife decision making is that choices should reflect the person making them and not simply manifest a reaction to external circumstances. They need to be made from the inside out rather than from the outside in.

People often question the external structure of their lives at midlife, and external changes concerning such things as relationships, lifestyles, and work are sometimes necessary. However, these major life changes are best not grabbed as quick solutions, but rather should be taken as invitations for in-depth self-evaluations. The external changes that do take place at midlife are healthiest when they result from inner self-exploration. People too often have made career or relationship changes at midlife only to find out later that the career or relationship was not the primary force behind the change.

While, as Jung says, the primary task of young people is to engage the world and find a place in it, the primary task of older people is to become their true selves and shape their worlds with their uniqueness. Young people need to look toward their outer environments to build a strong identity (ego) by learning to make a living, by forming relationships, and by securing a place in the social order. Older people, who have completed some of these outer world tasks, need to expand their identify by looking inward to discover the pieces of their personalities that are not yet developed. They need to move toward their own wholeness and develop their own uniqueness. Rather than searching for a place in the world, they need to shape the world with their own special unique contributions. In other words, they need to provide wisdom.

The shift at midlife from the external to internal orientation—from the focus on external structures and events to self-reflection—can feel threatening at first, especially in a fast-paced, nonreflective society. It requires that people slow down enough to consciously explore their thoughts and feelings, ideas, sensations, and imagination.

Many people worry about the process of self-exploration and where it might lead them, perhaps uncovering painful memories or resulting in depression or isolation. Some feel that the use of time and energy for self-exploration is selfish. Still others are concerned that this inner focus will deplete the energy they need to deal with the external world, fearing that they will be unable to keep their "edge" at work or keep up with their responsibilities. There is the potential for withdrawing too much, but for midlife people to deny themselves the opportunity to examine the meaning of their lives simply because they are busy not only leaves them not knowing who they are and what their lives are about but also leaves them dependent on external circumstances and other people; it denies them the opportunity to share their maturity and wisdom with others.

The process of looking inward is subjective and slow moving. One client spoke of the pace of his midlife transition as follows: "I was 37 years old. It took me ten years to get to the point where I had walked through midlife transition enough to identify what was going on." Another client spoke of how she "slept with it every night and lived with it every day. Every morning I'd say, 'How can you still be here? Go away!' But it didn't." People who value efficiency, strategizing, goal setting, outcomes, and speed often have difficulty dealing with the patience, endurance, and lack of assurance that one must cope with during midlife. There is simply no quick fix. A quick fix for this process is dangerous and will not work.

Despite the demands of this process, people at midlife must continue to live their lives and to go on functioning. They must maintain their focus on their external lives while patiently turning inward and waiting for understanding. Not only must they wait and listen, they also must trust the inner voice that comes. In a society that values the external world as much as ours does, this represents a significant task.

Yet successful midlife transition requires some degree of listening and trust of one's inner voice. One woman described her experience of gaining inner understanding as follows:

> It's a knowledge that's sure, but it comes from the gut....The facts aren't there to support it; all that there is is the feeling that you've hit it right on and you've got to do something about it. You've got to move with it, and you will become the person you are being called to be if you move this way.

Authenticity and Community

The demanding discipline of inner exploration and coping with the inability to find quick solutions and clear direction, as well as the sense of loss that is often experienced during midlife, can be difficult for many people. Additionally, people often describe feelings of being misunderstood and a sense of isolation, especially from their community. There is a fear that their community might demand conformity rather than support their authenticity and individuality. There may also be a sense of isolation from work, institutions that have supported them, and societal norms. Rarely are institutions or organizations willing or able to deal with people experiencing midlife transition.

For some, this process of separation can be minimally disconcerting; others feel it as a death experience, suffering from loss of such things as relationships and the assurances received from religion, jobs, income, status, prestige, and self-confidence.

It is important to acknowledge the cost of true self-understanding and the pain of isolation people experience during the process. In her struggle with her midlife vocational choice, one woman needed to separate from her friends. She explained to them that she just couldn't be with them, that she had to use the time she might be spending with them for other things. In explaining her feelings about her friends at that time, she described how they were "mucking up the water and cluttering up the business....What I had to take care of was me."

As necessary as self-exploration and withdrawal from others is, it creates difficulty in relationships and work as well as within one's own psyche. To say that maintaining relationships during midlife transition requires work, patience, and faith may be a gross understatement. Yet it is sometimes the midlife experience that provides the necessary opportunity to address such unfinished matters as ungrieved deaths, abuse, and lost opportunities—not to mention anger, envy, aggression, and other aspects of the so-called darker side of human nature. All of these things may stand in the way of the midlife journey.

Unexplored Aspects of the Self

Though it is sometimes painful for people experiencing midlife to explore and discover unresolved issues and their *shadow*, the Jungian term for repressed or undeveloped aspects of personality, these new pieces of oneself are often interesting and inviting. Accepting that as they first appear they can evoke strong responses such as anger, guilt, anxiety, and sexuality, it should also be said that these aspects can also free up energy and can be the key to feelings of wholeness. They represent the missing parts of ourselves, and they can offer renewal and promise. Murray Stein (1983) speaks of this discovery process as "the return of the repressed":

> When the unconscious erupts at midlife, what first comes most strongly to the fore are rejected pieces of personality that were left undeveloped and cast aside sometime in the past, for one reason or

another, in the rapid movement forward of personal history. Life still clings strongly to them. And actually the seeds of the future lie in these neglected figures, which now return and call for restoration and attention. (p. 78)

This dynamic was illustrated for us by a woman who told us how her mother's sudden death led her to claim her feelings, a previously rejected part of herself. She explained that before this time, she repressed any emotion, not wanting emotion to get in the way of any accomplishment. The repressed emotions that emerged at the time of the death flooded and almost sank her. Yet after integrating them, she was able to describe this painful process as a "gift" that enabled her to live at a deeper, more authentic level.

Another woman experiencing midlife explained her realization that she had lost all sense of self-confidence, which she attributed to her attempted suicide. Speaking of her dysfunctional marriage, she said, "I was in a situation where I had no right to an opinion. I was never right. I had completely lost my self-esteem, my self-confidence." With the help of others, she came to realize that she did not have to be taken advantage of, and it led to the breakup of her marriage. The breakup was difficult and painful, but she explained that through the process she had regained her self-assurance and ability to cope. Her connection with her sense of confidence, a part of herself that she had lost, made the future seem possible.

Personality strength, or *ego* in Jungian terms, is essential to the difficult process of integrating the previously undiscovered aspects of personality with the known ones. People must have a sense of who they are and have some ability to cope before they can safely and effectively deal with what has been repressed or undeveloped. They need to know who they are before they can begin dealing with who they not yet are. Yet growth at midlife often follows confrontation with what we don't know about ourselves rather than consideration of what is already known, emanating most often through weakness rather than strength.

Integration of all aspects of personality—the familiar and identified parts as well as the shadow, repressions, and other undiscovered aspects—

calls for a strong heart. Integration is about balance—the need to balance new insights we gain about ourselves with our existing understanding of who we are. This is rarely an easy process. In fact, midlife can be a time of excess in that we may cling too long to the old worn-out parts of ourselves or embrace the new at the expense of the old. But neither extreme is successful. Midlife development demands an end to either/or thinking. It leads to both/and thinking. This expansion of personality, this movement toward becoming all of who we are is movement toward individuation and spiritual growth.

Developing New Spiritual Values

Though never perfectly or completely, integration and movement toward wholeness do occur in successful midlife transition. There is always a shifting of perspective, sometimes readily observable in external realignments, sometimes barely perceptible in internal realignments. This shift of perspective can lead to a focus on a new set of values that are primarily spiritual, as Jung helped us realize. These values concern such things as discovering one's true self—or the spiritual within each person—and living in relationship to that true self in the everyday world. These values also concern a connection to others, a connection to the source of values, and a connection to everything in the natural world. These new values concern seeing the meaning and purpose of one's own life and how one's own life is part of something bigger and grander.

With the establishment of such values, feelings of discontent, confusion, loss, fear, grieving, and questioning lose some of their urgency, though they may resurface. People come to realize that they can know themselves and understand that their lives do have meaning, direction, and purpose, both for themselves and for others. They come to see that they are in fact the carriers of meaning in the world, that their journeys are not only individual personal journeys but also journeys for their societies. This spiritual task of attempting to discover and to stay in touch with one's true self and inner voice is a difficult and ongoing one.

One must find one's inner voice and relate to it, though blind obedience is not what should be sought. Rather than blind trust, a strong relationship and careful dialogue with one's inner voice may be best. The ego, the center of one's consciousness, is still responsible for decision making, but once it is connected to the self, the spiritual source, it no longer stands alone. It is now connected to something much greater than itself. And not only must the illusive inner voice be discovered and related to, it must be brought into congruence with one's external life.

This will to be authentic and congruent is something that most of us desire, and the movement toward this goal is more than personal. Paradoxically, as we come to be in touch with our true inner self, we find we can be in touch with those around us. Isolation then fades and true community can be established. In a real sense, we can come to know that to some degree when another person fails, we all fail and that when another person succeeds, we all succeed. In his book *The Well and the Cathedral*, Progoff (1977) speaks eloquently of this sense of connected-ness, which can be a part of any individual's journey during midlife transition:

> The metaphor of the well represents the individuality and
> uniqueness of our life, but the further we go into it the more
> completely we transcend the separateness of our ego-existence.
> It expresses the profound paradox that the more we move inward
> into our privacy and individuality, the more we become connected
> to the wholeness and richness of the universe. At its deeper levels
> we experience an expansion of consciousness that enables us to
> feel we are not limited to being only ourselves. We move through
> the well of the Self into a dimension beyond it, and that is when
> we come to the underground stream. Here we experience the
> Unity of Being and are one with it. It is the place of transcendence
> where, after a long inward journey, self-transformation and renewal
> begin. (p. 166)

In successful midlife transition, community is reestablished, but it is a community of separate, independent individuals, not of dependent people who cling to each other, hold each other up, adhere to collective mandates, and exclude those who disagree with them.

As one finds oneself and one's relationship to others, one finds meaning, mission, purpose, and direction. Fear and judgment diminish.

In *The Undiscovered Self*, Jung (1958) speaks of the importance of seeing one's own story in a bigger perspective:

> I am neither spurred on by excessive optimism nor in love with high ideals, but am merely concerned with the fate of the individual human being—that infinitesimal unit on whom a world depends, and in whom…even God seeks his goal. (p. 113)

One woman speaking from her experience also struggled to name her sense of spirituality:

> I don't even know the label for this, but I really believe that a spiritual dimension touches every aspect of our lives and it is up to us to stand in the middle of it and to be reflective about it—to know what's happening. We may not put a name on it: we may not be able to identify it, but we've got to know that that's what is going on.

With this awareness of meaning and purpose, successful midlife transition can lead us to know ourselves and how we want to live. We can come to understand what is ours to do and what we want to leave for others. Life can be lived meaningfully, spontaneously, and compassionately with emotion and a feeling of connection to oneself, to others, and to the natural world.

These general dynamics of midlife are shared by all types of individuals, though they are manifest in different ways. We will now turn our attention to a discussion of psychological type, and an exploration of how people with different psychological type preferences experience these general dynamics.

~~~~~~~~~~~~~~~~~~~~~~

Chapter 2

The Lens of Jungian Typology

We are naturally disposed to understand everything
in the sense of our own type.

C. G. Jung

Jungian Psychological Type Theory

Jung's theory of psychological type developed out of his twenty years of observing, analyzing, and attempting to understand the significant differences he found among individuals. Jung's extensive observations of patterns and recognizable differences in his patients, colleagues, and acquaintances constantly intrigued him and eventually led to his development of the theory of psychological type, expanded and made increasingly accessible by Isabel Briggs Myers with her development of the *Myers-Briggs Type Indicator* personality inventory. Psychological type can help us identify a process through which we can recognize and frame the characteristics and interactions of the basic elements of individuation for ourselves within the pattern of our own journeys. Jung described psychological type as a compass that helps us determine which functions we orient primarily to the outer, or *extraverted*, world and which we keep primarily for our inner, or *introverted*, world. He saw the four functions in the shape of a cross that includes both a rational axis (thinking/feeling) and an irrational axis (sensing/intuition), as the figure on the next page illustrates.

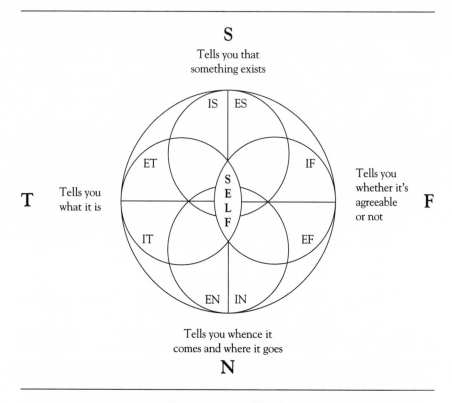

Compass of the Psyche

Words from *Man and His Symbols* by C. G. Jung, 1964, p. 61. Copyright 1964 by Anchor Press.

The four functions circle around the self, the image of personal wholeness. "I would not for anything dispense with this compass on my psychological voyage of discovery....I value the type theory for the objective reason that it provides a system of comparison and orientation which makes possible something that has long been lacking, a critical psychology," said Jung (1971, p. 541).

As an astute observer of human behavior, Jung was constantly intrigued both by the similarities and recognizable differences he observed in people. His image of the compass helps us identify which functions we orient primarily to our conscious or our unconscious world.

The Myers-Briggs Type Indicator

The *Myers-Briggs Type Indicator®* (MBTI®) is a personality inventory developed by Isabel Briggs Myers and Katharine Briggs. It identifies the sixteen psychological types proposed by Jung's theory. This inventory provides a powerful framework for self-understanding and for the appreciation of differences in others. Based primarily on Jung's ideas about orientation and consciousness, the MBTI instrument is a tool that can broaden our framework for understanding our own personalities and those of others, including how we interact with and view the world. It maps out sixteen basic paths of development, while also allowing for differences within each. People who wish to take the instrument must have it administered by a trained professional such as a psychologist, counselor, some clergy members, or others who have met qualifying criteria.

In this chapter, we will present psychological type theory as represented in the MBTI.* As similar themes become apparent among people who have a similar psychological type, we can raise hypotheses with increasing accuracy about the characteristics of people with specific psychological types at midlife. However, we must recognize that these are frequent patterns we have observed and will not apply to all individuals who have the same psychological type code.

The MBTI reports preferences on four distinct scales: *extraversion* or *introversion*, indicating whether people get their energy from the outer or inner world; *sensing* or *intuition*, indicating whether people perceive the world primarily through their senses or through intuition; *thinking* or *feeling*, indicating whether people make decisions based primarily on objective logic or on personal values; and *judging* or *perceiving*, indicating whether people prefer a structured, orderly way of life or a spontaneous "go-with-the-flow" way of life. Though people of all types use each of the eight preferences, each person prefers those that are most comfortable and which require less conscious effort to use. Jung believed that traditionally

---

* For further discussion of the *Myers-Briggs Type Indicator*, see *Gifts Differing*, *Type Talk*, and *LifeTypes*, which are listed as references and resources at the back of this book.

one preference on each dimension was dominant throughout people's lives, providing a habitual way of reacting to the world.

Extraversion and Introversion

Jung initially identified the opposites of extraversion and introversion through his attempts to understand significant differences between himself and Sigmund Freud, his mentor, colleague, and friend for many years. His book *Psychological Types* is devoted primarily to understanding these opposite preferences.

We all use both preferences at different times and focus our attention on the external and internal world. But we all have a tendency to be more energized by one or the other and prefer to spend the majority of our time focusing on either the extraverted or introverted world. Jung acknowledged that everyone had a preference for either extraversion or introversion, but he also recognized the need for people to integrate both attitudes in order to achieve balance. When people are drained of energy, they may need to return to the world in which they are most comfortable. As is the case with all the preferences, there should ideally be some sense of balance between extraversion and introversion, and part of one's midlife task is to learn how and when to use each of them appropriately. A person's preference on this dimension reflects the primary direction of his or her energy flow.

Our energy for life, therefore, comes primarily through either our inner or outer orientation. Finding a comfortable balance enables us to access both our inner and outer worlds. Jung was aware of the need for these different orientations to exist in harmony with each other, although he recognized the difficulty most of us have in finding a rhythm that works for us. The need for inner-outer balance, therefore, helped Jung understand our natural inclination to orient ourselves primarily toward either our internal or external world.

Extraversion (E)

Extraverts tend to draw their energy from the external world and are energized by people and activities. They tend to adapt quickly and comfortably to new environments and external activities. They give out energy and in turn receive energy back from others. They cultivate energy givers, including people, activities, gatherings, interactions, and other forms of external stimulation. Because they respond to situations as they are, their actions often precede reflection. External objects or situations are like magnets that draw in the extravert. Extraverts tend to have large networks of friends, acquaintances, and co-workers. They expand their lives by belonging to many organizations and groups, from which they receive recognition and energy. They may express thoughts, ideas, intentions, and feelings with conviction, sorting through and clarifying their ideas as they speak. They tend to learn more about an issue or what is most important to them by talking things through, processing them aloud, and receiving feedback from others. In Western society, where extraversion is highly valued, extraverts generally find their outer focus encouraged and rewarded. By frequently showing their extraversion, they receive affirmation from others as they continue to use, refine, and develop this preference. Interactions with their outer environment tend to be comfortable, stimulating, and exciting.

Introversion (I)

Introverts receive their energy from their inner, subjective world—a world that cannot be directly observed by others. They are reflective and need time to ponder and consider a situation before talking about it or acting on it. A pause often precedes a response or action from an introvert. The extravert's energy givers—people, activities, and gatherings—may act as energy depletors for the introvert. Even if introverts have momentary surges of energy in "people" settings, they often feel drained once they are away from the situation. Introverts tend to reveal themselves to only a select few. Their internal gauge decides where, under what circumstances, and to whom they will reveal themselves in the external world. Introverts are energized by their own reflections, insights, emotions, and internal worlds of ideas. Much of the dialogue related to their thoughts, ideas, intentions, and feelings takes place internally and is so strong and seems so real to them that they may believe they actually shared their ideas aloud to others. In reality, only a small percentage of it is externalized. For this reason, introverts often need time to focus on what they're going to say before they speak so they have a chance to rehearse before responding.

Sensing and Intuition

In addition to having primarily either an extraverted or introverted orientation, people also have two preferred ways of perceiving the world and judging what is perceived. According to Jung, the mental functions of sensing and intuition are simply two different ways of taking in information in the world around us.

Sensing (S)

Those who prefer sensing perceive the world primarily through conscious perception of sensory data—what they see, hear, touch, and feel— which Jung identified as the conscious ways in which people perceive both external and internal physical stimuli. The focused awareness of sensing types on their environment often enables them to become aware of aspects of their environment that may elude others. Conscious of their physical surroundings, they are literally "grounded," aware of the space they move in. Their imagery tends to be earth-based, and they focus on the present moment, the here-and-now, initially receiving and accepting what is without questioning or elaborating on it. This often includes an awareness of the signals they receive from their own bodies, especially in the case of extraverted sensors. Their physical responses often clue them in as to how they are reacting to the things they see or hear.

Sensors like to find a practical use for ideas and objects, using their imagination as a way to "dream the possible dream," and focus on what seems practical and relevant to them. When they get an insight, they often tend to dismiss it, possibly missing what might be important data. Because they are grounded in reality, they apply their ideas to their present situation, change it a little bit, and then move on.

Sensors tend to apply what M. J. Kirton (1987), in his *Adaptive Innovation Inventory* (KAI), calls *adaptive creativity*. Those who are creative in this way tend to generate a sufficient number of well-chosen and relevant solutions to things that they can refer to when necessary. Sensors usually support existing paradigms, focusing on using them better and more efficiently.

Sensors often achieve clarity by focusing on what they think is most important. They find that too much extraneous data can prevent clarity. Frustrated by ambiguity, they may find complexity difficult. Too many disconnected details or facts can leave them feeling confused and overwhelmed. Their insights don't exist in a void; they need to have a framework, connections, and guidelines. A general idea, especially one that they perceive as unrelated or out of context, often seems inadequate to them. Ideas, concepts, and theories need to be presented in a context or framework that has an obvious structure of beginning, middle, and end. They need a summary of the main parts and connections of things before they can look at other possibilities or the more nebulous parts of things. Focusing enables them to concentrate on the task at hand, to bracket things out for a particular moment, thus enabling them to keep their minds on the present. They like to collect, sort out, and organize facts and details, and then decide which ones are relevant. To be acceptable to them, symbols and theories need to be connected to reality or first-hand experience. Sensors tend to see things as they are, accepting and appreciating their reality and molding them into concrete shapes and figures.

Intuition (N)

Intuitives tend to become aware through their unconscious perceptions, making connections that cannot be traced back to or validated by any conscious sensory observations. More like a sixth sense or a hunch, intuition seems to appear "out of the blue" from a gathering place in the unconscious, leading to an "aha" experience in the conscious. Though often unaware of the source of their perceptions, which may appear as a gestalt, intuitives learn to trust their validity, even though they may be unable to determine or explain how their perceptions come into existence. In conversation, intuitives tend to jump from one point to another, assuming that their listeners can make the appropriate connections between their thoughts and fill in the necessary gaps.

Intuitives usually tend to prefer what Kirton calls *innovative creativity*. They often redefine problems, focusing on doing things differently and on creating new paradigms. Because they often challenge existing operating procedures, they may have difficulty working in highly structured organizations. Extraverted intuitives are good at brainstorming and making connections in the outer world. They are often seen as "idea people" who are able to look at situations from many points of view. They become energized by all the ideas being passed around, and their contagious enthusiasm stimulates the process. Introverted intuitives, with their intense amount of internalized ideas and hunches, may find it difficult to formulate these ideas into words and communicate them to others, and perhaps even to themselves. If they cannot explain the source of their perceptions to others, they may come to doubt their own experience or not share their ideas with others, or at least exercise extreme caution before discussing them. When involved in a brainstorming session, their best ideas may come to them after the meeting is over.

Thinking and Feeling

Once people have taken in information, either through sensing or intuition, they reach closure or make judgments about it through the rational decision-making processes of thinking or feeling. Jung believed that every judgment a person made was conditioned by his or her personality type and that every point of view was necessarily relative. Thinkers and feelers generally use different criteria to make decisions.

Thinking (T)

Thinkers judge data and reach conclusions based on objective data. Their focus on reasoning enables them to base their decisions on analysis, logic, cause and effect and consequences, and the criteria of justice and fairness. They are adept at formulating questions, creating theories, and challenging ideas. Often critical of themselves and others, they enjoy analyzing situations and information, challenging what they see as inconsistencies and flaws, and striving toward objective logical conclusions. Performance oriented, they prefer to be appreciated for what they do, their logical analysis, the products of their efforts, and the results they produce.

Thinkers may have difficulty getting in touch with their emotions and often need help describing the symptoms caused by their emotions, which are often physical, and identifying the possible emotion behind them. They may need to translate their feelings through their objective thinking process before they can identify them.

Feeling (F)

Feelers tend to use their own value system to attach values to the data they take in. They accept or reject ideas, situations, or individuals based on what is most important to them. They may be very critical of those who do not live up to their cherished values. Jung stressed that feeling was a rational decision-making function, since he felt that feelers could be aware of the process of how and why they made specific decisions. They are, however, more likely than thinking types to consider their own emotions and the emotions of others as relevant data for decision making.

Harmony is most important to those with a feeling preference. They tend to be uncomfortable with conflict and often try to ignore it or restore harmony before they have fully dealt with the issues behind the conflict. Those with a feeling preference share much of themselves in relationships. If they push their preferences to an extreme by always being available to others, they can run the risk of losing their own sense of who they are. For feelers, being appreciated for what they do is not as important as being valued for who they are. They often experience conflict between their dual desires to be true to themselves and to please others.

Judging and Perceiving

The preferences of judging and perceiving are considered attitudes. Isabel Briggs Myers (Myers & Myers, 1980) made the observation that "judging types believe that life should be willed and decided, while the perceptive types regard life as something to be experienced and understood" (p. 69).

Judging (J)

Judgers tend to be decisive, preferring closure, completion, and structure in their outer world. For them, there is a place for everything, and everything needs to be in its place. Life is to be decided, willed, planned, and organized. They prefer to control their environment by planning ahead, structuring their lives around schedules that enable them to

24

prioritize their work and ensure that the "work" will get done accurately and on time. They understand the way things "should be" and may become frustrated when others don't comprehend or value their need for structure and organization. They tend to be list makers, crossing off what has already been completed and often adding past tasks to cross off so they can experience a further sense of accomplishment and closure. Even their "free" time may be scheduled, so that they can have sufficient time for "spontaneity" in their lives. They are quite comfortable in organizational and societal cultures that provide structure, value and follow stated guidelines, and focus on adherence to the rules and regulations that ensure a structured, efficient, and well-operated organization.

Perceiving (P)

In contrast, perceivers tend to be open, curious, and adaptable to whatever changing situations they encounter in their environment. Focusing on a "grab bag" of possibilities, they enjoy going with the flow and experiencing life as it is happening in the present moment. In their outer world, they tend to be open ended, responsive to the moment, and frequently subject to change. They often have many projects going at once and enjoy the variety and challenge this offers them. Those who work within an organizational structure are often frustrated by the constant, inherent rules, regulations, and deadlines. Things will get done, but within their own time frame. Their open-ended, flexible, and emerging lifestyle enables them to be responsive to the needs of the moment and the different, rapidly changing cultures around them. They have a tendency to put off making decisions. Aware that more data is always available, they prefer to explore the infinite possibilities that might exist before being tied down to one concept or option. For them, all decisions are tentative and subject to revision if and when new insights and information surface. They believe life is made to be enjoyed with all its flexibility, potential, and new possibilities.

Using Type Theory to Reach Self-understanding

We have found the MBTI personality inventory to be personally illuminating, intellectually challenging, and theoretically exciting. It identifies a pattern of development for each type, a lifelong process of growth and unfolding of all that people are capable of becoming. Each of us uses all eight preferences. However, as Jung indicated, one preference on each scale will be used more comfortably and will be more natural for each person. Jung's theory of psychological type helps us focus on our continuing journey toward wholeness into the second half of life, when we learn to incorporate at least some dimensions of the preferences not in our type and thus are able to achieve more balance in our journey toward wholeness.

Socrates' familiar injunction to "know thyself" provides the core of Jungian type theory. We need to understand and continue to assess our own development in order to clarify our strengths and weaknesses. Increased self-knowledge of our preferences and how we use them will not eliminate all confusion and misunderstanding, but it may lessen our need to project our own desires and weaknesses onto others, while also validating who we are as unique individuals. We must continue, as Jung did, to remind ourselves that every judgment that we make is conditioned by our personality type and that every point of view is necessarily relative.

Our type preferences provide us with a road map for the first half of life, a path for developing our type to the best of our ability. Sometimes true preferences are difficult to determine, especially if one is introduced to the MBTI instrument at midlife, when development often becomes increasingly focused on the preferences not in one's type code. The second half of life encourages us to journey toward wholeness as we seek to integrate some attributes of those preferences not identified in our type code. Integration does not mean substituting, but adding to, and using the other functions appropriately.

Chapter 3

Viewing the First Half of Life

*The achievements which society rewards are won at
the cost of a diminuation of the human personality.*

C. G. Jung

Jung's theory of human development is based on the general framework
for the lifelong process of individuation—the process of moving toward
fulfillment of the unique potential within each of us.

During the first half of life, identified by Jung as the stage of *accommodation*, we develop an ego—our subjective, personal sense of who we are,
the center of our consciousness. As we move through childhood and
adolescence, we adapt to the external world, often deferring our sense of
self to the needs, requirements, and demands of others. We all need a well-
functioning ego that will help us select which thoughts, ideas, feelings, and
memories to allow into our consciousness and which ones to prohibit. The
selection process, filtered through the lens of our personality, helps us
focus on what is most important so that we are not overwhelmed by the
vast array of available data and stimuli. Our ego is composed of both
personal and collective material, with content that is unique for each
individual, time frame, and culture. As we continue to build and expand
our ego, we identify with an increasing number of individuals, groups, and
organizations. The natural connection that occurs during early childhood
between our ego and self—our image of wholeness, what is often referred
to as the *ego/self axis*—is often broken during accommodation as we

internalize messages from individuals, groups, organizations, and a variety of other sources. This is a time for making choices between equally valid options and selecting options at the expense of forfeiting others.

As we receive guidance from others, we often follow a collective path, adapting to external expectations of family, community, group affiliations, geographical location, culture, race, gender, social context, and the historical period in which we live. For most of us, accommodation requires various degrees of adaptation to the outer world. We listen to and identify with external messages from our families, and from communities, peers, teachers, TV stars, group affiliations, and heroes, who often influence our choices. These models influence our image of who we would like to become. The roles we "select," therefore, often cause us to identify more with our adaptive selves and thus may unconsciously continue to influence us long after they have ceased to be appropriate.

Jung (1933) recognized both our need to make choices as we adapt to such expectations and the dangers of doing so. "In my picture," he said, "there is a vast outer and an equally vast inner realm; between these two stands man, facing now one and then the other, and, according to his mood of disposition, taking one for the absolute truth by denying or sacrificing the other" (p. 120). In our complex modern world, we often find ourselves bombarded by numerous and often conflicting messages from a wide variety of sources. The choices we make are only partially conscious—some are well thought out, some are designed to please others, and others are made by default.

The Adaptive Persona

As we accommodate to meet the expectations of others, we also "choose" certain roles that are identified through our relationships to various individuals and groups, such as son or daughter, student, athlete, friend, scholar, worker, and leader. Jung identified these different roles as our *persona*, consisting of a composite of the various roles or masks of adaptation that enable us to conform to specific situations and environments. The concept of persona, meaning "to sound through," dates back to ancient Greece, when it referred to the different masks worn by actors of the Greek theater. Each persona contained a small megaphone to amplify the actor's voice and more clearly reveal the actor's character and expressions. Because theaters were located on the steep slopes of Athens, undoubtedly few members of the audience could see the changing expressions of the actors. Thus, the persona, or mask, was originally designed to amplify and more clearly reveal character.

Jung described persona as a "complicated system of relations between individual consciousness and society, fittingly enough a kind of mask, designed on the one hand to make a definite impression on others, and on the other, to conceal the true nature of the individual" (De Laszlo, 1959, p. 162). Thus, like the Greek actors, we also "dress up" for our roles as manager, teacher, business executive, minister, parent, and so on, by assuming the appropriate costume, social facade, demeanor, and language for each of our roles. Increased awareness of our various personae can help us make more conscious choices regarding when, where, and how to use our roles appropriately.

Adaptation of our ego helps us relate in positive and acceptable ways to the outer world and to those around us. Early on in the process of social accommodation, we may experiment with different roles as we identify with certain movie and television stars, literary characters, teachers and other role models and as we "take on" some of the qualities of others to see how they fit us. Our persona also incorporates the numerous "voices" in our heads and the messages that relate to each of our roles. Thus, we may internalize many of the messages that arise from the external expectations of parents and friends, group affiliations, societal norms, and the mass media. Our roles amplify who we are, defining us in terms of such things as a loving parent, a committed partner, a trusted friend, a creative person, a competent manager, a spiritual seeker, and a change agent. Through these outer roles, we gradually develop stable and reliable ways to interact with others. The persona we choose often represents a compromise between who others expect us to be, who we would like to be, and who we really are. Although some roles require more energy than they give back, we may continue using them because of our values or commitments. By selecting certain roles, we also rule others out, which may then be reintegrated during midlife to expand our opportunities for increasing growth and development. Our persona has both positive and negative sides, as the table below illustrates:

Persona

Strengths	*Limitations*
• Enables us to interact with and be accepted by others	• Conceals our inner self from others
• Provides means for public recognition	• Promotes inappropriate use of certain personae
• Promotes advancement and favorable responses in specific situations	• Allows overidentification with specific roles at the exclusion of others
• Conceals parts of ourselves we prefer not to have or reveal	• Decreases awareness and understanding of self
• Provides reliable ways to relate to others	• May give mixed messages to others
• Allows for more automatic, comfortable responses	• Ignores negative impact on others
	• Denies parts of ourselves

Changing our persona to meet the expectations of individuals, groups, and society may reflect more of our actual need to follow the examples of other individuals, groups, and organizations through our accommodated selves than our need to validate our own uniqueness. Therefore, just as the mask can amplify our personae, it can also hide who we really are. When we rely on specific personae, we often become overly identified with certain roles, to the exclusion of other potential aspects of ourselves. Jung stated that Western society often places more value on achievement and persona—the "doing" self—than it does on personality and individuation—the "being" self. If we become overly attuned to the "should" and "ought" messages that we receive from others, we may no longer have a sense of our own uniqueness. Instead, the face our ego presents to the world may reflect more the old messages we received from others—the path of the collective—than it will our own inner selves. Who we are in our private inner worlds may be quite different from the public face we present. When we play a role to gain love, respect, and recognition from others, we may consciously or unconsciously hide who we really are and thus never feel that we are loved and respected for our true selves.

~~~~~~~~~~~~~~~~~~~~~~~~~~~~~

Chapter 4

Close-up of the Midlife Journey

*When the soul awakens at midlife and
presents its gifts, life is permanently marked
by the inclusion of them.*

Murray Stein

Now that we've looked at the ways in which we accommodate to the external world during the first half of life, we will examine the midlife experience that follows. When midlife happens, some do not recognize it as a major turning point in their lives until they look back on it. For others, the transition is more clearly identified as a "crisis," with the characteristic symptoms of a crisis.

Symptoms of Crisis

- Stagnation
- Despair
- Depression
- Regression

- Inner malaise
- Isolation
- Loneliness
- Paralysis

This part of the journey may be viewed more positively as an opportunity for new growth and development, as shown on the following page.

Crisis as Opportunity

- Seeds of new beginnings
- Growth
- Integration of the shadow
- Gifts of the unconscious

- New energy for life
- Enjoyment of the present
- Enthusiasm for the future
- Moving toward wholeness

The Chinese ideogram for crisis combines the characters for danger and opportunity. Although both are an inherent component of any crisis, we often recognize only the danger at first. Upon later reflection, we may come to understand and value the possibilities of new directions that often occur from periods of crisis, and are then able to recognize the potential for new beginnings that would not have been possible before.

It is during this period that people often ask themselves the most basic questions of life:

- What is the meaning of life?
- What am I missing?
- Is it worth the effort?
- Have the choices I've made taken me where I really want to go?
- Can I afford to make some different decisions at this stage of life? What are the consequences of doing so?

- What is my life leading to?
- Where do I go now?
- What personae am I using and are they right for me?
- What are my alternatives? Will they really enhance my life?

These issues may lead to intense questioning and a symbolic reversal of the values we held during the first half of life. These crises of authenticity often cause many people to reevaluate their lives and make more conscious choices regarding the second half of life. People in midlife also experience a conflict between some basic polarities that Jung has identified as endemic to human experience. People frequently feel pulled in two

Danger

Opportunity

Chinese Ideogram for "Crisis"

very different directions at once—toward their past, which is already familiar to them, or forward into a direction that may be new to them or in contradiction to their orientation during the first half of life, thus creating tension, doubt, and questioning. The polarities listed on the following page were identified by our workshop participants and clients as things commonly experienced during the midlife transition.

Frequent Polarities Common to Those in Midlife

Old patterns/new meanings	Turmoil/rest
Expansion/constriction	Fright/exhilaration
Very rich/very empty	Either-or/both-and
Completion/change	Regrets/yearnings
Attachment/separation	Entrapment/freedom
Dominant/inferior	Confusion/clarity
Inner/outer	Masculine/feminine
Personal/public	Loss/new beginnings

At midlife, people need to realize that what is most important is for them to find their own stories, modifying or discarding messages from the past that are no longer appropriate and clarifying the things that continue to be. Midlife requires us to move away from Jung's period of accommodation and to travel through three stages, identified by Murray Stein as the *rite of separation, rite of liminality,* and *rite of reintegration,* before moving toward Jung's stage of individuation. An explanation of each of these stages forms the organizing framework for the remainder of this chapter.

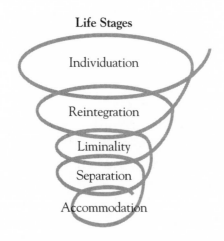

Life Stages

Individuation

Reintegration

Liminality

Separation

Accommodation

As the figure indicates, a generally linear, forward-moving progression from accommodation through midlife to individuation is likely to occur. However, within any of these stages, individuals may find themselves retracing their steps, caught in unresolved dilemmas, revisiting old issues—though often from a new perspective—or feeling stuck and immobilized. They may continue to repeat former self-defeating patterns that, while familiar, can also often be damaging. Stein (1983) recognized that these regressions, which often repeat old themes, tend to increase our awareness of unconscious material and may lead to a deeper understanding of who we really are.

Rite of Separation

During separation, the first stage of midlife, we begin to separate from our ego, the conscious part of ourselves that identifies who we are to ourselves and to others. This rite of separation focuses on the breakdown of the persona—the carefully cultivated masks that represent our collective roles, values, and expectations. We often need to question the appropriateness of some aspects of our persona when our roles change and certain masks or roles don't seem to fit our lives anymore. Midlife compels us to reexamine our persona carefully to see which masks are still appropriate and which ones need to be modified or discarded. Comparing the amount of energy we expend on our most active personae to the amount of energy we receive in return can be helpful during this transition. For some roles, expended and returned energies may be balanced; for others, there may be significant discrepancies. Even with an imbalance, however, we may decide to continue certain roles for a variety of reasons—the immediate costs of change may be too great, we may fear that eliminating one role may also eliminate other important roles, the benefits of keeping the role may outweigh the disadvantages of doing so, or a particular role may be a stepping stone to something more desirable. For other people, recognition of the imbalance may lead them to make changes or eliminate certain positions entirely.

If we do choose to retain roles that no longer provide us with much positive energy, we needn't just hang on to them, but we should recognize what choices we have. We may also need to establish some balance through the various personae that continue to energize and nurture us. When the breakdown of roles, triggered either by external and/or internal events, leaves us hanging in suspension and questioning who we are, we may begin to search for new roles that are more appropriate for the second half of our lives.

People in the separation stage of midlife may also experience the "loss of a dream," as Daniel Levinson (1979) calls it. The intensity of this loss is perhaps most desperate at midlife, when our earliest images of who we would like to be and where we would like to find ourselves by the time we are forty may be quite different from the reality of our lives.

We may recognize that our images of reaching our professional goals, living happily within our marriages, or establishing warm, loving relationships with our parents will never be realized—or, at least, not in the ways we had hoped or expected. We may even have reached our goals—professional and/or personal—only to find that the reward is bittersweet. People may find themselves asking, "Is this all there is?" In a society that often defines people by what they do and who they are in relationship to others, separation can be a traumatic experience for people. People may ask, "If I'm no longer a spouse, child, parent, next in line for promotion, or president of this organization, then who am I now?" Separation is a time of loss that causes us to grieve—for our past, for our dreams that may never materialize, for our lost youth and our increasing physical limitations, for our aging or dying parents, for our adult children leaving home to make their own lives, for feeling as though we don't fit into traditional patterns anymore, and for relationships and organizations that provided us with stability for many years.

We also come to realize that we're closer to "old age" than we once thought would be the case, and time seems to be running out. Some people in the stage of separation experience an increasing sense of isolation, along with a concern that other people don't really understand them. Others make precipitous changes that they later regret. And still others feel as though they are stuck on a treadmill, unable to find a way out. Further complicating the issue is a feeling that one doesn't even understand one's own experiences. Although all may seem well on the surface, below the threshold everything may be seething with uncertainty, fear of change, and questions about oneself, which brings into question everything that was accepted during accommodation.

Some of the major tasks of separation include the following:

- Breaking down of one's persona
- Grieving for the past and unrealized dreams
- Learning to bury the past and move on
- Finding an appropriate balance between grieving and moving on
- Increasing one's recognition of opposites

- Recognizing inevitable life changes
- Forgiving oneself and others for past mistakes
- Becoming aware of potential new roles
- Identifying roles that primarily reflect the expectations of others

Midlife can be experienced in varied degrees of intensity, depending on one's personality, support systems, current job stability and enjoyment, spiritual support, and past experiences with crises. For some people, separation can unsettle the very foundations of their lives, as one man described:

> Last night, I dreamt that the pressures of life had enclosed
> me in a cage. As I stood there, I felt the walls pressing in on me,
> moving slowly closer and closer. I stretched out my arms to push
> them away, but they kept moving in. I called out for help, but no
> one came. I couldn't seem to catch my breath, as fear and panic
> escalated within me. I suddenly heard myself scream as I awoke,
> my body trembling and sweat pouring down my face.

This man's dream reflects the intensity of his midlife experience and his feelings of immobilization, as he felt his life was falling apart around him.

For other people in midlife, separation can be more subtle. The way individuals react to such transitions often depends on external and internal events, including their own unique patterns of dealing with crisis, how much control they have over the changes they are experiencing, the presence or absence of appropriate support systems, and their personalities.

Without understanding the dynamics of the separation stage, people may continue to feel immobilized as adults whenever they are confronted with old and familiar societal and parental messages. Separation forces us to reexamine the internal messages we have consciously gathered to determine whether they are still appropriate for us as adults.

In summary, the separation stage of midlife often releases a flood of intense emotions for many people—grief and anger for what has been lost, fear of a future that is unknown, feelings of depression, resistance to change, disillusionment with life, rationalization, denial and blame, and physical and emotional exhaustion. These emotions can often be overwhelming and immobilizing. Many people find themselves feeling vulnerable and exposed during this period. "The razor that leaves your soul to bleed," as the line from the song "The Rose" puts it, is an apt description for how many people are left feeling during this stage of midlife.

Rite of Liminality

Stein identifies the rite of *liminality* as the central experience of the midlife journey. In Latin, *limen* means threshold or doorway, a borderline space, betwixt and between. Liminality encompases a sense of disorientation, fragmentation, alienation, ambiguity, paradox, and drift. A yearning to return to familiar and more secure space often conflicts with a pull toward challenging new directions. Questions arise regarding the necessity of the journey. Most of us have little choice. Both internal and external forces move us on the path toward individuation.

Stein compares "psychological floating," an essential aspect of liminality, to a boat whose anchor lines have been cut. At the mercy of the waves, the boat rocks back and forth with no sense of direction, floating on uncharted waters. The disorientation and drift people often experience in this in-between space can pull them back toward what is familiar—though often painful and no longer appropriate—or move them forward into the unknown, with its uncertainty, promise of potential renewal, and challenge. We often find ourselves between personae—torn between who we believe we have been, who we currently believe ourselves to be, and who we believe we have the potential to become. Letting go of certain personae may be necessary, though painful. Many of us may decide that restructuring and reinterpreting our current roles is possible and more appropriate during this period. The feelings of floating, instability, and confusion, though a natural part of the liminality journey, are difficult for everyone, although people may experience the uncertainty with different degrees of intensity. With our boundaries no longer secure, we often feel emotionally vulnerable and susceptible to previous messages and patterns, even when they are no longer appropriate.

Liminality brings us closer to our unconscious, which may offer its gifts of deeper understanding and awareness, along with the unfolding of previously unavailable potential. During this stage, people frequently feel torn between the battle of their ego-consciousness—their sense of who they are now—and the latent potential waiting to be discovered. Dreams, inner images, and daydreams, which may be especially vivid during liminality, may offer an understanding of liminality in symbols and help us identify new directions.

Common questions that arise during the liminality stage include the following:

- If I change my role—who am I?
- How do I know what to discard and what to keep?
- How can I avoid making precipitous decisions that I will regret later?
- Will I ever get out of this?

- What will become of me?
- What new aspects of my persona do I want to embrace?
- How am I going to get where I want to go?
- What directions should I move in?

When in the stage of liminality, people should try to remember that the potential for both danger and opportunity is inherent in all crisis situations. In midlife, conflicting pulls toward integration of the psyche and the potential paralysis may threaten to keep people stuck in either the past or the present, unable to envision any way into the future.

As we have discussed, liminality is a period of psychological floating that can cause people to feel disoriented and confused as they struggle to regain their footing. Letting go of parts of themselves that no longer fit is both a necessary and painful step toward individuation. As we move into the reintegration stage of midlife and the second half of life, we may increasingly value the past, with both its pain and its contributions to the development of new life.

Rite of Reintegration

Unlike the trauma that often characterizes the period of separation, the shift from transformation/liminality to the *reintegration* stage of midlife may be nearly imperceptible. Our sense of liminality gradually becomes more comfortable. The landscape is transformed, and we realize that the contrast between the heights and depths has diminished as a gradual leveling takes place. Our roles continue to change, and we become aware that some of the intensity has faded. By the time we reach reintegration, we have become increasingly accepting of who we are and the directions we have chosen.

Many people at this stage of midlife still find themselves clinging to personae they carefully developed earlier in their lives, even though they may no longer be appropriate. At this stage of life, people may need and want to reintegrate some of those parts of themselves that they have previously relinquished.

Reintegration includes the integration of a personal, inner search, along with an enriching sense of relationship with others, identifying companions on the journey, and a deepening sense of connection with the spiritual. We must also continue to honor the need for liminality, that state of psychological floating that keeps us flexible by maintaining a sense of receptiveness and openness to continued growth, new possibilities, and new directions.

Reintegration calls us to reevaluate our persona, to make more conscious choices regarding how and if we are going to continue our various roles and which roles we should modify or replace. We may choose to weed out roles that reflect more of our accommodating selves and to focus on those that connect us more deeply with our true selves. By integrating more appropriate personae at midlife, we may experience increased inner coherence, or a sense of "coming home," as we pay less attention to the collective voices of the outer world and focus more on our own inner knowing.

Some of the key tasks of reintegration include:

- Knowing and validating our home base

- Experiencing inner renewal

- Redefining goals

- Focusing on a spiritual center

- Communicating between the ego and the self

- Having access to both inner and outer worlds

- Continuing to integrate opposites

- Being open to continued development

- Sorting out what still fits and what needs to be changed

- Reaching congruence of roles

- Validating the inner self

- Retaining some sense of liminality

- Increasing the access to our unconscious

- Connecting more deeply with the shadow

- Feeling greater harmony with the rhythm of life

As mentioned, reintegration involves a shift in focus from ego and persona to self. Stein sees reintegration as a time during which we distinguish between our former sense of how we and others have seen us through our persona in the past and the new individuals we are becoming. Reintegration helps us accept loss and grief and move on with increased understanding and new awareness to validate our own experience, embracing our own stories, and shifting our focus from external to internal authority.

Reintegration invites us to recycle around our psyche to integrate the undeveloped parts of ourselves. Recycling of our psyche is especially necessary at midlife so that new growth, creativity, and versatility can emerge and so that our personalities will not become stagnant. Our continuing development helps us move toward increasing balance through the lifelong process of finding a sense of equilibrium and the integration of opposites—ego/shadow, anima/animus, conscious/unconscious, and other archetypal patterns that may be activated in our lives at various points in time.

Reintegration also requires increased awareness and understanding of those aspects of ourselves that continue to create problems for us. Continuing to integrate unconscious material, a central task at midlife, can also occur with intentional inner work through journal writing, meditation, prayer, active imagination, imagery, personal counseling and therapy, and focused reflection. Each of these methods can expand our consciousness and lead us to a greater understanding and appreciation of ourselves.

During the reintegration stage of midlife, people often experience some of the following beneficial changes:

- A decreased need for pretension
- An increased incorporation of learnings from projection
- An increased integration and comfort with opposites
- A deeper sense of a spiritual connection
- An increased authenticity
- A greater appreciation and acceptance of others
- An ability to value and enjoy our own uniqueness
- An increased fulfillment of life

For each of us, some aspects of the journey are solitary and unique, since reintegration results in a move from collective guidelines to our individual path by helping us focus on our personal journeys.

Focusing on Renewal and Spirituality

Renewal and a deepening focus on spirituality are common and pertinent reintegration themes. During reintegration, many people recommit themselves to the religious expressions of their childhood and adult lives, finding a richness in the traditions that continue to speak to them. Others, who find that they no longer feel comfortable with the traditions they may have learned, seek new and/or expanded expressions of their spiritual lives. As already indicated, Jung recognized that all of his midlife patients sought some kind of spiritual outlook on life. Those in midlife whom we've counseled continue to confirm Jung's assertion. Reintegration at its deepest level focuses on spirituality, however it may be defined.

Jung concluded that when answers to the problems and complexities of life do not come from within, they mean very little. "Outward circumstances are no substitute for inner experiences," wrote Jung (1965, p. 5). He recognized the spiritual search for meaning as an integral part of his own psychic experience and encouraged others to see it as the same. At midlife, we each must hold up the mirror that reflects ourselves, exploring questions that resonate with our deepest sense of who we are.

As we shift from the outer world of accommodation to an increased focus on the inner spiritual world at this stage of midlife, Jung believed that we seek deepening connections with the spiritual, which he believed was our ultimate source of meaning. This continuing process of development, with its integration of polarities, enables us to become increasingly centered and whole and more deeply connected to our spiritual side, to others, and to everything around us. These growing connections can fill and enhance our personal journeys by integrating the dimensions that resonate most deeply within each of us, enabling us to experience and know for ourselves, as Jung put it (1933, p. 122).

Jung believed that the main task for people at midlife was to recenter their lives around a new set of spiritual and cultural values (Hall & Nordby, 1973), values that are often neglected during the accommodation stage of life. He saw the spiritual dimension, as symbolized in the *mandala* through the integration of opposites, as an integral part of our psyches that offers us unique images of who we are. "The mandala is an archetypal image which signifies the wholeness of the self," wrote Jung (1965, p. 334). Jung was intrigued with mandala images, sacred circles whose four-fold symbolism of psychic integration represents wholeness and completion, the union of opposites, and the path to individuation— the lifelong process of becoming whole. He recognized the symbolism of the mandala through the myths of different religions and cultures, his personal experience with dreams and his own unconscious, and the many dreams of his patients. In his autobiography, *Memories, Dreams, and Reflections*, Jung (1969) discusses his own process of exploring his journey. Each day he would draw a mandala that reflected his unconscious, wondering where this process would finally lead him. He eventually recognized that, for him, the mandalas were leading back to the center— the midpoint—pointing toward individuation:

> I began to understand that the goal of psychic development is the self….There is no linear evolution; there is only a circumambulation of the self. Uniform development exists, at most, only at the beginning; later, everything points toward the center….The center, therefore, is the goal. (pp. 196–199)

Jung was also intrigued by the medicine wheel. His research, personal visits, and continuing correspondence with Mountain Lake, chief of the Pueblo tribe in Taos, New Mexico, increased his understanding of the Native American's use of the medicine wheel with its inherent symbolism and healing power. Hyemeyosts Storm (1972), in his book *Seven Arrows*, describes the importance of the imagery of the medicine wheel as a sacred symbol of their life journeys in the ancient culture of the Plains Indians. To create a medicine wheel, small stones or pebbles are carefully placed on the ground in a circle by the medicine man, conveying an image of the total universe, recognizing both polarities and harmony between the opposites. Each stone is equal to one of the many realities of the universe. For the Plains Indians, the relationship between human beings and the world is expressed most completely by the concept of a cross within a circle. Thus, the medicine wheel reflects the four directions within the continuity of the encompassing circle. The four directions of the wheel correspond to aspects of the four mental functions identified by Jung, indicating both their strengths and weaknesses. The north refers primarily to thinking, the south to feeling, the east to intuition, and the west to sensing and aspects of introversion.

In summary, after we each have found our "beginning place" during accommodation at the first half of life, we need to move toward integration of the other dimensions of the mandala or medicine wheel at midlife, to learn the lessons and wisdom of each direction. As Storm writes:

> At birth, each of us has a particular beginning place within
> these Four Great Directions on the Medicine Wheel. This Start
> will be the easiest and most natural throughout our lives. After
> each of us has learned of our Beginning Gift...we then must grow
> by seeking understanding in each of the four Great Ways. Only
> in this way can we become Full, capable of Balance and Direction
> in what we do. (p. 6–7)

Individuation: The Path Toward Wholeness

In his Seven Arrows' medicine wheel, Storm writes about the necessity of integrating attributes from each of the "Four Great Ways." Jung identifies this developmental path through the framework of the four mental functions—sensing, intuition, thinking, and feeling. He recognized that this path was part of a spiritual journey, which he called *individuation*, referring to both the goal and the lifelong process through which each of us becomes a separate, unique individual.

As was explained earlier, people tend to accommodate during the first half of life, exploring who they are by following the societal guidelines set forth by the family, religious institutions, and various other groups that people belong to. As we have seen, during accommodation our egos often become separated from our selves, as we focus on certain parts of our personality at the expense of others. During this stage, we focus on selecting certain appropriate personae that enable us to meet, or accommodate to, external expectations. A central task of individuation is to restore what is called the *ego/self axis*, the natural connection between our own image of who we are and our true individual potential. When this connection, which is often weakened during accommodation, is strengthened through increased communication between our inner selves and our accommodated selves, we can relate more fully to our own selves. As we move into the second half of life, we learn to reevaluate our identity and to discover and honor our own uniqueness.

Although he identified individuation primarily as an internal process, Jung understood that the process also presupposes a collective relationship, not isolation. We must achieve balance between our inner awareness, our relationships with others, and our involvement with the world at large. We need to value our uniqueness, with both its strengths and weaknesses, and offer our gifts to the world, as we seek wholeness through our inner journeys and our relationships—both of which can help us identify, understand, and value individual differences.

The natural, inner process of individuation encourages us to recognize, own, and eventually integrate the often conflicting polarities within us—the ego and self, opposing personality characteristics, our conscious and unconscious, our potential for good and evil, our inner and outer focus, and our personal and collective selves. The tension between such opposites reminds us—sometimes gently and at other times quite dramatically—of the growing dimensions of our personality. Jung also saw the task of individuation as a time to incorporate all our psychological preferences to be available as needed—not developed equally, but used appropriately. The more we increase our awareness and understanding of ourselves, the better able we will be to move toward individuation and wholeness.

Jung recognized that individuation, though influenced by collective thoughts, values, and patterns, is primarily an intensely personal journey that for the most part must be traveled alone. This contrasts with the collective path that is typically followed during accommodation. Jung saw individuation, not as a self-centered path, but as a search for balance in which both self-understanding and connections with others interact and enhance one another. The path may be linear, or, increasingly at midlife, may be seen as a circular and often spiraling pattern that periodically recycles around the psyche with a different focus to clarify issues and enable us to view our life experiences from new perspectives.

As we each continue on our path toward integration, we are encouraged to seek an appropriate balance between the external messages we receive from individuals, groups, organizations, and our cultural backgrounds and the deep, inner wisdom that resonates deeply within each of us, as the chart below indicates.

Achieving Balance

Accommodation	*Integration*
• External authority	• Internal authority
• Parental and societal messages	• Inner messages
• Focus on persona	• Focus on the self and individual uniqueness

Understanding the Psyche

Jung's understanding of the psyche presents a framework for personality type and various other aspects of his theories. He saw these theoretical constructs not as realities in themselves but as guidelines that describe what is not directly knowable—as tools to illuminate our own experiences. The psyche, Jung's word for personality, reflects both our conscious and unconscious, centering around the tension between opposites and our lifelong task of integrating opposites.

Our type preferences straddle the boundary between conscious and unconscious. Sometimes they are more easily available to us, at other times tripping us up. The ego represents our identity, our image of who we are in the world. During the first half of life, our ego tends to be in charge— orchestrating the many ways in which we connect with the world around us. In typological terms, the ego is primarily composed of the four preferences in our type codes. Our ego determines what will be admitted into consciousness and what will be ignored. As we increase our comfort and skill at using the functions in our type codes, we often do so at the expense of their opposites, which tend to settle into our unconscious world, where they often remain primitive, childish, and undeveloped. Our type preferences also influence what parts of ourselves we accept in our ego and persona, as well as what we reject and cast into our shadow. We tend to listen to messages from others during the first half of life. As symbolized in the model of the psyche depicted on the following page, the boundaries between conscious and unconscious, and between personal and collective unconscious, are porous, allowing for exchange.

Jung believed that we are each born with a self—an image or blueprint of our uniqueness, identified as both the center and totality of our psyche. As an inner, organizing center, the self moves us toward a synthesis of opposites, the different and often conflicting parts of ourselves, through the process of individuation. We have seen that a primary task for many of us at midlife is to separate from the "collective" and to alter or discard messages that no longer fit our lives. Therefore, when the former image of ourselves is shattered at midlife, we may need to focus on rebuilding a newly emerging sense of who we are.

Jung (1965) identified the self as "the principle and archetype of ori- entation and meaning" (p. 199), which contains the "seed" of our po- tential growth through our own unique path. He derived the concept of the self from the religious thought of India, but gave it the specific meaning of the total personality, which includes the eventual integra- tion of opposites. From this "seed" comes the fullest expression of our individuality.

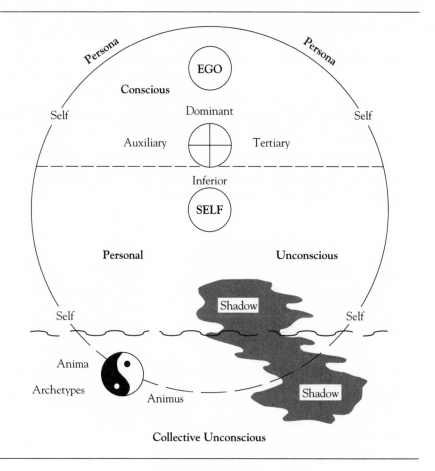

Model of the Psyche

Fancy Warrior (Frank Davis), a Native American elder of the Pawnee tribe, described his path to understanding as "a trail filled with scraps of paper, each a piece of the puzzle. 'Pick up each scrap and save it,' he said. 'When you have many scraps, pull them out to read. If you live long enough, there may be enough information to help you understand some of the wonders of life'" (Wall, 1989, p. 56). The MBTI personality inventory and Jung's model of the psyche and the individuation process provide us with tools that can help us decifer the "many scraps of paper" we each collect along our own path of individuation.

Jung's model of the psyche provides a lens that can help us identify both the differences and commonalities that occur during the midlife journey and relates these differences to other dimensions of the psyche. An increased awareness of the similarities and differences that can occur during the journey can help us to validate and enhance our own paths, while also enabling us to honor the paths of those whose worlds are often quite different from our own.

Part 2

Stories of Midlife Journeys

Chapter 5

Typological Gifts and Challenges at Midlife

*We shall not cease from exploring. And the end of
all our exploring will be to arrive where we started
and know the place for the first time.*

T. S. Eliot

As we explore, we view everything, including midlife transition, through
our own eyes, and how we see things is determined by our own psychological type preferences and our life experiences. When we consider that our
experiences are affected by our past and current relationships, our
affiliations and environments, as well as our personal interests, abilities,
values, socio/educational/economic levels, physical and mental health,
and other factors, it may be easy to assume that people have little common
ground for describing midlife, or any other common life experience,
for that matter. But this is not entirely true. Even in the face of overwhelming differences, people who have a similar personality structure
do report consistent themes in their life experiences. If used with
care, psychological type codes can serve as an organizing principle for
helping people examine, and ultimately make sense of, their midlife
experiences.

In this chapter, we will look for patterns in people's midlife experiences,
and we will begin to plot the midlife transitions of people who represent
each of the sixteen types identified by the MBTI personality inventory.

We will look at "typical" midlife issues associated with each type as they have emerged in our work, including retirement, career changes, changing family roles, and changing values and expectations.

Most of the people who shared their experiences with us through workshops, retreats, classes, questionnaires, and interviews were approximately between the ages of 35 to 50 years old at the time the observations were made, and they were all aware of their type codes. The material in this chapter represents neither the worst nor the best aspects of any one type, and should help to illustrate both the gifts and challenges that each type faces during midlife.

The material in this chapter is organized by pairs of like-dominant types (e.g., extraverted intuition, introverted thinking, extraverted thinking, etc.), and material for each pair of like-dominants is presented in several ways. First, "typical," and therefore necessarily limited, profiles are presented to illustrate particularly common, ordinary, everyday midlife issues faced by a particular type. These profiles are then followed by analyses and observations that place the practical situation described in each profile in a more theoretical context. Then a broader presentation of descriptive material is offered for each pair of types to illustrate the issues that typically arise as people of these types move from the first half of life to the second half. In this discussion, the "typical" midlife experience of each type is discussed in general terms, addressing such issues as how a particular type's tendencies and common behavior can affect a person's midlife experience. The critical steps and adjustments that people of this type can make to reach enriched self-understanding are also included, as are the benefits and positive changes that often occur as people of this type face and cope with their midlife transition. And finally, there is a summary chart for each pair of types that identifies how midlife transition is characterized for the types, what relationship issues emerge for these types during the midlife transition, and how people with these types can be helped through their midlife experience by others. Those close to the person experiencing the midlife transition are given specific suggestions and guidelines for how they can help people of this type with their midlife experience.

Keep in mind that the material in this chapter is composite in nature, not the experience of any individual, and while it is true, it is not complete. Rather, it should be taken as suggestive and should not be limiting in its applications.

Profile: ISFJ

Mary wanted to talk about a dream. That was a surprise to her friend, for Mary did not typically talk about dreams.

"In the dream," she began, "I went to a hospital to pick up my newborn baby. Upon arriving there, I found the baby to be ill. In the dream, I took it to a medical office where I found my children's pediatrician and my religious leader dressed as doctors examining another child. Neither of them even acknowledged our presence. I took the baby home, not knowing how to care for it, but nevertheless determined to do so."

Mary seemed to have her life together. She appeared competent and extremely neat, though at times she also seemed restless, overcommitted, and tired. She had a loving family and lived in an attractive home. Her friends thought of her as "poised"—as responsible and caring—and as the kind of person who coped well with life's ups and downs. They would have been surprised to learn of her dream images of ill babies.

Mary in fact saw herself much in the way that others saw her. She told herself that she was quite fortunate and that other people had lives that were much worse than hers. She didn't talk a great deal about her life because she thought it would bore other people, and she also wasn't convinced that talking would help her anyway. Besides, she was too busy to talk about things. There was so much to do, so much she should be doing, and so little time.

"Why," she wondered aloud to her friend, "being as fortunate as I am, does life seem so lacking in joy? Why am I always worried? Why do I feel confined and bored? Isn't there something I'm supposed to be doing that I'm missing? I've always had this question of what I am to do, but since my children have grown up and my parents have died, it seems more and more important. In fact, I'm almost obsessed with it. It haunts me. I must get some clarity about what my mission is before time runs out. I would give anything for clear direction. Everyone tells me that I look like I have it all together, but some days I feel my life will fly apart. It's as though I'm holding on tightly and I'm not sure how long I can hold on. I'm so tired."

"What must you hold onto?" her friend asked.

"Something. I must hold onto something," she responded. "My work, maybe. Yes, I must hold onto my work. What I do is important. If I don't do that, what will I do? My work helps me know who I am, and I must hold onto some idea of who I am. And the structure of a workday keeps me sane. I must hold onto my family, too. They are important. And I suppose I must hold onto the church—though I can't bear its pat answers, and its demands make me weary. If I don't hold onto something, I'll drown."

Mary, who seemed to others to be as solid as a rock, was trying to stand upright and remain unmovable as the rising water swirled about her, demanding change. She felt that she had to keep her feet on solid ground, that she must hold on. She felt that she must keep things under control or she would drown. No wonder she was tired. Clinging so tightly could make anyone tired. Trying to keep things in boxes that are too small, boxes that have been outgrown, could exhaust anyone.

Mary knew her life was changing, but she hated confusion and she abhorred disruption. She feared change and avoided risks. And she worked at understanding herself. She read self-help books—every book anyone recommended. She attended seminars and classes and she sought the help of teachers. No effort was too great.

What might happen if she were to relax and stop trying so hard, if she could think of what she wanted, rather than what she thought she should want? What would happen if the protector of collective institutions and values and faithful caregiver were to stop protecting and caregiving? What might her life be like? Perhaps some of her frantic busyness, her searching, and her weariness might be blocking her from her best source of direction and clarity.

Mary's friend asked her what might happen if she were to relax and, for a short time at least, stop trying to plan her life and manage her world and instead just observe her life and accept what she found. Mary couldn't imagine this. As was the case in her dream, she felt unseen.

Mary was quiet for a while. Then she asked, "What if I find that what is required of me contradicts everything I've been taught?"

Summary of Observations: ISFJ

- Mary's dream breaks into her everyday world to announce that help is not in the form of external authority figures.

- Mary's persona of calm and stability masks her inner turmoil and deeply felt needs.

- Mary fails to recognize that her own boredom, confinement, weariness, and lack of joy are signals for her to let go of the obsolete patterns of her life and seek a deeper level of understanding.

- Mary retains her gifts of persistence and diligence.

- Mary now feels abandoned and uncared for after years of fulfulling the roles of faithful caregiver and keeper of values.

- Mary realizes that it is painful to let go of the symbols of stability and community that she has always honored.

Analysis: ISFJ

An important dream lays out Mary's situation and her problem. In the dream, Mary has given birth, and her newborn child, or new life, is in need of help. She takes her need for help to the places where she has always found assistance before—to external authority figures represented by the medical profession and the church. But this time the external healers are not equipped to help her. Mary has sought help in the wrong place. She will have to find help in a different place.

Finding this different place proves to be extremely difficult for Mary, for she has always honored conventional wisdom and time-honored traditions and institutions. And now she has expectations of them. Traditions and institutions give her guidance and a sense of safety. She feels it is arrogant for her to question their authority, and she is terrified of being without the predictable and reliable paths they offer her. The rules, directives, institutions, and authorities have kept chaos at bay, and Mary fears chaos. Yet all around her life is changing. Old ideas just don't seem relevant. Boundaries are too tight; previously accepted compartments are too small. She feels overwhelmed, afraid, and anxious. She hates confusion, disruption, and discord, and she feels abandoned and deserted by those who won't (or can't) help her. She is angry with those who don't offer to help her, and she feels lonely.

In typological terms, Mary needs to develop some of her less developed preferences. She also needs to honor her introversion, which she has sacrificed, as do many ISJs, in successful efforts to organize and manage her world. In some respects, her attempts to make things happen in her life have cost her the ability to find her own direction and purpose. Her constant involvement in activity has denied her time to reflect and has cut her off from her best source of personal data.

Mary could also benefit from developing some intuitive skills and learning how to trust them. Intuition, especially extraverted intuition, can lead her to broaden her view and to enthusiastically embrace alternatives. Doing so may painfully destroy her sense of focus and clarity, but it may also lead her to consider alternative views, perhaps even ones that sometimes diverge and conflict. In these conflicting views she may discover the inadequacy of narrow authority sources that proclaim one solution or one path to a problem. She may come to see the limitations of "shoulds" and "oughts," even to the degree that she will challenge whether they continue to have validity in her life. For her, however, there is also danger in relying on intuition too much. Too much fluidity and too little grounding might leave her feeling exhausted. Honoring her down-to-earth sensing, with its measured, careful attitude, can provide safety during such times.

Mary will also need her feeling and thinking functions to help her evaluate her new options. Her extraverted feeling function (her auxiliary function) is well developed. She understands what others want and need from her and knows how she can meet their needs. Her introverted feeling function is not so easy for her to access, yet she will greatly benefit if she can find a way to it. Her introverted feeling function can help her recognize what she values as well as what others want her to value. It might help her include herself in her own circle of care. And if her thinking function can be developed, she can come to see the consequences of choosing alternatives and making choices based on them, rather than making choices based on what she takes in from external, publicly proclaimed authority figures. She might come to understand the limitations of individuals and institutions, such as her work, family, and church, to meet her needs. She might even be able to bear the pain that comes from others failing to meet her needs, even to "see" her, as occurred in her dream.

Her thinking function, along with her sensing function, can bring much desired clarity to her hazy intuitive insights. Perhaps her thinking function, with its tendency toward assertion and confrontation, can protect her from the predictable conflict she will encounter when she attempts to meet her own needs.

Mary's midlife task requires that she break her heavy reliance on external authority, that she learn to trust herself, and that she expand her way of seeing things. She may find that she feels closer to her center, less tired and worried, and more secure and free when she realizes that she can find her own way by listening to herself. Her sense of confidence, enthusiasm, clarity, and direction may return when she can face paradox and find her own truth—that solid piece of ground on which she can safely stand.

Profile: ISTJ

I know I'm young to be retiring, Jim thought to himself, but I've worked for this company for thirty-two years. Now that they've decided to reorganize and there's an option for early retirement, I'm going to take it.

Jim wanted to retire, but he also worried about this choice. He worried about finances, though things would probably be fine, barring some unforeseen emergency. He worried about the possibility of an emergency, though, and he also worried about what he would do with his time. For fifty-five years, his life had been structured for him. What would he do without such a structure? He didn't have hobbies like some people. He liked to travel, and he played a little tennis, but a person can't fill life with things like that. Maybe he needed to do some planning.

Despite these worries, Jim looked forward to having some time to himself. He looked forward to not having to work so hard. Just last week on a rare day off, he woke up in the morning and went outside for a long walk. It was a cold fall morning and he enjoyed the brisk breeze and looking at the changing leaves. Jim was surprised to discover how close he was to tears. When his wife noticed his emotion and asked what was wrong, he was embarrassed. He told her that nothing was wrong and that he didn't want to talk about it. His unwillingness to disclose his feelings hurt his wife, something he hadn't intended. They hadn't had much time together and he wanted to spend more time with her. Maybe they would be able to do some traveling once he retired.

Jim also looked forward to not having to manage his staff at work anymore. For years, he'd had to motivate and monitor them. Frankly, he was tired of it all and wanted to leave it all behind.

Feeling a little guilty, Jim thought, "I don't really care what those people do if I'm not responsible for them. I don't even care what my children do—within limits, of course."

But something was bothering Jim. Sometimes he'd wake up in the night wondering if he might just become a parasite. "The world needs a lot of things," he told himself. "How long can I just look at the leaves? I have no skills other than the ones I've been using in my job. Once I'm out, I can't go back. I worry that there's nothing else I can do. I already feel useless just thinking about it."

Jim decided to seek some counseling. After an initial interview, Jim's therapist gave him a group of psychological tests and exercises. She told Jim they might begin with tools that ask specific questions in the hope that they might find some skills, interests, and values he could claim. He had never done anything like this before and found the testing interesting. He looked forward to discovering new things about himself and hoped to find something to do that would be useful and pleasing.

Confirming some test feedback at their next meeting, Jim said, "I do like to do things with my hands. I've had a workshop for years and I work in it when I can."

"And what do you like to build?" his therapist asked. Jim hesitated for a moment.

She rephrased her question—"What *needs* building?"

An answer came quickly. "Houses," he then responded. "Houses for low-income people. Renovating old run-down houses to keep families together. That's what needs to be built."

Family and work were what were important to Jim. It would be hard for him to feel like a parasite doing work that kept families together and benefitted society in a way that seemed essential to him. Excited, Jim felt as though he were on to something.

Summary of Observations: ISTJ

- Jim's change is a forced one, but he accepts it in a no-nonsense manner.

- Jim's great need for security and structure, as well as his need to plan, demand attention.

- Jim's dominant introverted sensing is life-giving, but is viewed negatively by him.

- His sense of responsibility has taken a heavy toll.

- Testing offers the kind of security, structure, concreteness, and information that appeals to Jim.

- With assistance, Jim makes the connection between his values and his action plan for retirement.

Analysis: ISTJ

Jim's option of early retirement has offered him the opportunity to do just what he needs to do for his growth and development, but he feels guilty about exercising the opportunity—guilty about really being free. Retirement offers Jim the opportunity to rest, to give up what he perceives as heavy responsibility, to "lighten up," to rethink, and to play, but his need to produce, as well as his high need for security and structure, threaten to undermine this opportunity. He feels anxious and worried, and he fears the unknown. He feels guilty for not doing what he thinks he should be doing and for not being as responsible as he feels he should be. He cannot bear to become what he calls a parasite.

In typological terms, Jim's extraverted thinking (his auxiliary function) has served him well in his career, but it is his dominant introverted sensing that is offering him great joy now. The brisk early morning air, the changing color of the leaves, and the promise of having a slower, freer pace are now gifts to Jim. Like many ISJs (and introverts in general) who have been committed to work and responsibility, he had turned his back on his dominant introverted preference. Connecting with this preference now brings Jim so much joy that he feels sentimental, even teary. Not understanding his emotions, and finding his response embarrassing, he doesn't want to talk about it. He is shaken by how strongly his emotions can be triggered by the discovery of these new joys, yet he still has difficulty accepting them. He tends to view the very things that seem to bring him joy as nonproductive and useless.

Besides the renewal that his dominant introverted sensing can give him, he also needs his feeling function to help him identify what is of value to him. He needs to identify what he might *want* to produce. Jim, being as practical as he is, wants to produce what *needs* to be produced. His task is to determine which of all the world's endless needs he personally wants to respond to. He needs to work on a project that he values and can personally relate to, not one that just simply needs to be done. He will be less tired and stressed once he discovers what his work will be and what he can leave for others to do. Besides his work, Jim greatly values his family. He now needs to spend time with them with the sole intention of having fun together.

His extraverted thinking function has served him well in his work with decision making, priority setting, and supervision, but Jim's intuitive function can be helpful, too. If he can find a connection to it, it may open up some possibilities for him. It may help him make connections between what he values and what kind of work he might do. It might also help him link skills he has obtained with other areas of work he might pursue. It might help him understand that what he already knows—that he loves to work in his workshop—can help direct his retirement work. His intuitive function might bring him a broader view and a brighter, more optimistic outlook, eventually leading him to ideas for leisure pursuits as well as work.

Jim's midlife task requires him to come to know and trust things he cannot experience, see, or rationally explain, but which he knows in his heart and mind are true. He may be closer to his center and feel freer, more spontaneous, and less weary when he realizes that he is much more than what he produces, that he can trust himself to know what he needs and wants to do, that he can care for others without taking responsibility for them, and that he can honor his need for rest and play.

Typological Descriptions: ISFJ and ISTJ

ISFJ	ISTJ
Stabilize-harmonize-actualize	*We honor our commitments*
Dominant introverted sensing	Dominant introverted sensing
Auxiliary extraverted feeling	Auxiliary extraverted thinking
Tertiary introverted thinking	Tertiary introverted feeling
Inferior extraverted intuition	Inferior extraverted intuition

Introverted sensors use their dominant preference to become grounded, to appreciate the moment, to enjoy the experience of the here-and-now. Taking in information for them is like experiencing a multimedia presentation through the senses. Introverted sensors have an intense awareness of everything around them, and little escapes them. They take in data through their senses—often from several sources at once—not wanting to miss anything. These specific impressions, both external and internal, are then internally processed and stored for future use.

The external focus on production and their own sensing-judging temperament often makes paying attention to their inner dominant sensing preference difficult for ISJs. They often feel less of a sense of being confined and pigeonholed. Midlife for them becomes increasingly a time for "responding as I am led, rather than by the rules of life." Moving from external "shoulds" and "oughts" to an increased sense of internal guidelines can become freeing for ISJs. With fewer constricting categories and more fluid boundaries, they feel less of a need to do everything right and to be perfect. During midlife, ISJs often learn to use their sensing in a more playful way, though they may need to negotiate with their sensing-judging temperament to do so, learning to give up the sense of living out someone else's beliefs, lifestyle, and attitudes. They may need to plan or schedule their fun, but may then enjoy the moment for what it is, allowing for time to let things happen, rather than make them happen.

At midlife, they often experience a sense of relief at recognizing the wonder of their inner sensing, relinquishing the "shoulds" and "oughts" from the outer world. One ISJ described this as "experiencing the lasting strength that comes from within and depends on me rather than the outer or material world."

ISFJs

ISFJs, who extravert their feeling function, focus on pleasing others and living by other people's guidelines and rules. Type development for ISFJs means learning to trust the answers from within—their own introverted feeling and their own inner feelings and values. The focus shifts from need for external approval to increased emphasis on learning to be themselves, not merely a reflection of the way others see them. A commitment that was primarily external now becomes internalized.

By developing an inner sense of their own values and learning to trust them, ISFJs can also learn to use their thinking function to support what is most important to them, becoming more assertive about meeting their own needs. As they examine the consequences of their actions, they can identify the benefits and drawbacks of doing so, let go of the "shoulds" and "oughts," and move ahead. Further development of objective thinking skills can help ISFJs in their academic pursuits, in achieving advanced degrees, and in assertively emphasizing their own needs and projects.

During midlife, ISFJs may find ways to use their inferior intuition within their own familiar structure by exploring new ideas within a practical working formula. Group work may help spark new ideas that are more difficult for them to access internally. They may reduce stress by using their intuition to find their way out of uncomfortable or difficult situations by exploring various new options. They tend to be more open to new ideas that don't totally change things, but that modify them gradually. Their intuition may surface occasionally through their "wild" ideas, especially when they are brainstorming in what they perceive as a safe environment. Fantasizing about an ideal job, relationship, or situation may get them in touch with their own values without requiring them to arrive at complete and final answers. When they can give up some control while still maintaining some guidelines, they often become increasingly able to follow their instincts, even when they can't see the rationale of letting things happen rather than making things happen. A workable framework or guideline helps them find a place to attach their own ideas and approaches. Being aware of specific goals and directions gives them freedom within structure to go with the flow and see what happens.

ISTJs

ISTJs tend to focus on more objective data, while ISFJs focus more on subjective data. ISTJs often talk about having a vast internal filing system, variously described as a grid, a computer, or a catalog that is available for continuous storage and retrieval of minute details. It contains concrete, objective information and systems, along with feelings, clues about body language, and good or bad vibes about individuals or situations. They appreciate being invited to share their extensive amount of data. Their internal processing also informs them when something doesn't seem quite right, enabling them to access the necessary data to support their uncertainty. Their focused sensing helps them feel grounded, as they take in all the relevant facts, experience them for themselves, and recognize when something seems out of place. They want information to be presented in precise and explicit ways, and expect others to make their point without going off on tangents. Their sequential processing, therefore, moves in a very thorough and orderly way toward a conclusion.

In midlife, ISTJs may learn to integrate their feeling function by paying increased attention to their own identity. Some ISTJs may become sentimental as they grow increasingly aware of their emotions and learn to express them more fully and comfortably. They also recognize their growing need for support through ever-deepening relationships.

In midlife many of them often become less oriented to work, as they seek an increased balance between career needs and personal relationships. Having maintained the image of a tower of strength, they are usually very self-contained and outwardly composed, even as they become increasingly aware of their own vulnerability. Using their sensing may help them become more attuned to the needs and feelings of others, as well as their own feelings. When expressing emotions, they may become overly sentimental. At midlife, they often learn to extravert their feeling with greater ease.

The Midlife Transition: ISFJ and ISTJ

Introverted Sensing Style: The School of Shoulds and Oughts

ISFJ	ISTJ
Moving with fear and trembling.	Less is better.

Characteristics of ISFJs and ISTJs

- Inner and/or outer trigger events (initiators) that alter life structures
- An inner sense of constriction and need for expansion
- Feelings of worry, anxiety, pessimism, guilt, fear of change, discomfort with lack of clear direction, and fear of being overwhelmed
- Slow, careful, persistent, and measured pace
- Attempts to find clarity and move through transition "correctly"

Particularly True for ISFJs	Particularly True for ISTJs
Lack of confidence and fear of displeasing others	Distrust of anything not grounded in the physical dimension of life

Relationship Issues

Other people (depending partially on their own type preferences) may

- Feel they are stuck, negative, overly composed and controlled, and resistant to change
- Find them to be skeptical and demanding of assurance that the outcome of their midlife transition is "worth the risk"

Others should try to

- Understand their own needs and biases and be empathetic to the person's resistance to change and lack of certainty
- Appear worthy of their trust and loyalty
- Be sensitive to subtle, easy-to-overlook clues that indicate that they are ready for new options, changes, or risks

70

Particularly with ISFJs, others should	*Particularly with ISTJs, others should*
Provide support and gentle dependable direction if asked for it	Show respect for them and demonstrate their own ability to "live in the real world"

Guidelines for Helping ISFJs and ISTJs Through Midlife

Recognize and confirm the strengths of introverted sensors—their clear focus, preparedness, willingness to take suggestions, diligence, groundedness, and service orientation

Particularly with ISFJs, others should try to confirm their	*Particularly with ISTJs, others should try to confirm their*
Ability to know what is needed and to respond to it	Ability to see things "as they are" and to accept them

Encourage balance to introverted sensors (which will also help them develop their intuitive skills) by

- Encouraging calculated risks and measured releasing of status quo

- Encouraging the consideration of new options

- Encouraging questioning of outer authority and trust of self

- Suggesting a more expansive view and a less focused task orientation

- Encouraging trust of ways of knowing (i.e., fantasies, imagination, dreams, hunches) that aren't limited by what one can know through the senses

- Promoting recognition of the absence of absolutes—or the idea that there is "one right way" of doing things

Particularly Helpful for ISFJs	*Particularly Helpful for ISTJs*
Point out the danger of dependence and the need for discovering one's own path rather than the path one "should" follow	Point out the limitations of rationality and the pitfalls of discounting things and reductionistic thinking

Profile: ESFP

Maria was a large woman with slightly graying hair. The first thing that people noticed about her was her smile and easy, relaxed manner. People knew that when Maria was with you, she was really with you.

Today Maria talked with her spiritual director. "Things have changed since I was here before," she began. "I feel stuck, and I really want to get on with my life. I can't move; I feel like something's shifting. It's weird. I don't have any idea what it is all about, but it is happening. It feels like something is shaking me. I don't understand it, but it is real. This shifting has been going on for sometime, but it still feels unusual for me."

Before this time, Maria had described feeling like a robot. She had immersed herself in activity—whatever came along. She had felt as though she were wound up and moving in whatever direction she was pointed. Although she had accomplished a lot, nothing seemed to matter. She explained that she was once able to maneuver well, but that now everything was an effort for her. She wanted to stay involved and she couldn't stand not to be with other people, but she was not handling herself well. What was this shifting and seeming inability to continue her normal life all about?

Her director asked her what she thought it might be about. "I don't know what it's about," she responded, "but I want to do something about it. It feels uncomfortable. I want it to stop. It's controlling my life, and only I should control my life. I want to be free."

"What was it like to be a robot?" he asked her, trying again.

"It was like being wound up—like moving aimlessly—or maybe like moving where someone pulled me," she responded. "It was like I had no control, but it's over. I'm not a robot now."

Maria wasn't interested in talking about how she had felt like a robot. She wanted to talk about what was happening to her now. Now she couldn't move. Now it felt as though parts of herself were slipping away and she wondered what would be left. She had always been able to engage people and activities around her, but now she couldn't do that. Now she felt as though she were being pulled in.

Maria remembered another time when she'd felt she were being pulled inward. It was after a surgery she'd had the previous year. She'd spent two months recovering, and the recovery period had slowed her down. During the recovery, she couldn't do anything and spent much of her time alone, thinking about what was really important to her. Now she realized that maybe all of this questioning began then.

She realized that the feelings she had had after her surgery were not entirely pleasant. It had been a bad time for her. She had felt immobilized and a little depressed. She didn't want to go through that again, but she did want to feel in control of her life. She didn't like being immobilized. She also knew that if she could focus on the things she had discovered during her recovery—the things that really mattered to her—that she would feel more confident and less like a robot. She would simply make a new life for herself. There was no doubt that one of Maria's greatest gifts was her ability to act on what she knew.

Maria was surprised. She realized that she already had some of the answers she was seeking. She realized that she knew what mattered to her and that if she honored that, then she would know what to do to claim the meaning of life. She was ready to begin her new journey.

Summary of Observations: ESFP

- Maria's warmth and enthusiasm are genuine.
- Maria's sense of being shifted and her robot analogy bring questions about the meaning of her life.
- Maria doesn't want to continue discussing the robot analogy; she wants to get on with solutions and action for resolving her present conflict.

- Maria recognizes that the robot moved when external circumstances directed it rather than through her own control.

- Maria wants to focus on the present, not the past.

- Maria's surgery and subsequent recuperation enabled her to explore personal values that were impossible for her to undertake while her extraversion and sensing-perceiving temperament were totally in control.

- Maria's enthusiasm and optimism provide her with the energy and motivation to begin her journey.

Analysis: ESFP

Maria feels as though things in her life were being shifted and that parts of herself were slipping away. Though uncomfortable and immobilizing, this transition energy has stopped her "robotlike" movements, and offers her the opportunity to make a connection to her deeper self. If she can use her immobility, imposed originally by an illness, to search for a true, authentic connection to her inner values, she will gain clarity about the meaning of her life and claim some control.

This is hard for Maria, for although she previously felt uncomfortable when others were directing her, she could then at least maneuver in her world. She now feels that she has lost much of her ability to function effectively and that her energy is being "pulled in." Though it is because this is happening that she may be able to get in touch with her inner, personal values and eventually be able to control her life, it is still a difficult process for her. The interior world can be troublesome for anyone, but it can be particularly difficult for someone with a strong extraversion preference and an SP temperament style that desires action. It is especially so for Maria because it is the world of contemplation and she prefers action, because it doesn't communicate directly and clearly and she wants clarity, because it is a solitary place and she wants interaction, and because it sets its own pace, usually a very slow one, and she is in a hurry. It is easy to understand why she does not want to be pulled in. She is now more open to looking inward because she is having difficulty functioning, or "maneuvering," in her more familiar outer world.

Maria is very aware of what is happening to her. She needs to contemplate the meaning of what is happening, which has a purpose beyond the relief of her current pain. She is aware of how things are for her right now. She needs to also consider where things might be moving and what the purpose of the movement might be. She needs to see that she has an inner world to draw on whenever her external world seems unavailable and that her inner world can bring great joy. If Maria can find her connection to her inner source, she will use her dominant and natural gifts to share her newly found wisdom with the world. Her work will benefit her and many other people whose lives she will touch.

In typological terms, Maria especially needs to focus on her introverted feeling to discover what really matters to her and her thinking function to discriminate and prioritize those things. She also needs her introverted intuition to find the confident grounding for her future and her wholeness. Her extraverted sensing, with its orientation to the outer world, and her SP temperament, with its orientation toward action, have denied her the benefits of inner contemplation and reflection. Her tendency to take action combined with the relational quality of the feeling function have done her a great deal of good, yet this combination has also created the robot who has become problematic for her.

Her introverted feeling function might provide Maria with some access to her inner life and some means of evaluating her options. As is the case with many extraverts in an extraverted society, Maria's personal values have been overshadowed and her choices made with less authentic data. Her relational and value-oriented stands have been directed more by outer figures and events than by her own center. Her introverted feeling function offers her a way to find these values, but it demands a great deal of time, as well as awareness of hunches, memories, fantasies, and reactions to life experiences. Her introverted feeling function, with its capacity for memory, can add to her present orientation the wealth of meaning hidden in her past experiences. If she can focus less exclusively on the volume of outer voices, she may be able to hear the quieter, inner voice and come to trust its authority.

Her thinking function is also important. It has the capacity to evaluate and judge the outcome of potential actions. It may also help her prioritize and weigh the consequences of her actions, both to herself and others.

Her intuition can also help her break away from her tendency to be too oriented to the present and "things as they are." Her intuitive function can help her understand the meaning of what is happening in her center and give her glimpses of present and future possibilities. Introverted intuition can accept "what is" as a launching pad for what might be. It can also offer vision and breath and new data—often half-formed, inexact data that must be carefully evaluated with the help of her thinking and feeling functions. While it may not be a very trustworthy or controllable aspect of Maria's conscious personality, it may nevertheless lead her to see connections so that she doesn't have to "reinvent the wheel" and keep herself in constant, tiring meaningless activity.

Maria's midlife task requires that she slow down her pace and resist her tendency to take quick action and instead pay attention to what really matters to her. She will move closer to her center and feel less robotlike and more in control and directed when she recognizes the authority of her inner, as well as her outer, reality and when she comes to see the multitude of meanings that her experiences suggest for both the present and the future.

Profile: ESTP

Keith was an attractive, athletic-looking stockbroker who gave the impression that he was always in a hurry. He claimed that his wife, an INTP poet/teacher, had asked him for years to undertake counseling, talking endlessly to him about "psychological type" and "growth" and "their relationship," but somehow he had never really gotten around to making an appointment. Now, however, he was in a counselor's waiting room because Joan had informed him that if he didn't do something, she would leave him.

Keith explained to the counselor that he felt that his work supported his family well. "Joan and I have two fine children, a nice home, and a boat," he explained. "We sail in the summer and ski in the winter. I like to hunt also when I can. Why can't she be satisfied with this? She used to be. For years, she was teaching and raising our children, and on weekends we had fun. Now the children are gone, and all she is interested in is writing poetry and reading psychology books. She talks about herself all the time, and she wants me to talk about myself. I'm tired of it. She doesn't like to be with our sailing and skiing friends anymore. We don't have fun like we used to."

As Keith reflected on this situation, he realized that he was furious about it. Her attitude, he felt, was messing up their lives together. Keith didn't hesitate to express himself.

"Could it be that you're angry because you feel you're being forced to change or lose something?" his counselor probed.

"Sure, that's obvious," he responded. "To avoid losing her, I might have to become like her, but I don't want to."

"Of course you don't," his counselor responded. "And probably she can't be like you."

"Okay," he said, "I'll buy that, but what do I do about it?"

"How much is your marriage worth to you?" his counselor asked.

Keith was surprised at the question, but he knew the answer. It was worth a lot. They had children and a life together, and they had had a lot of fun for a long time. He knew he cared for Joan, and he knew the marriage was worth some time—time devoted to discovering how and why things had changed for them. It was worth time to find out how they both felt and what they both wanted and needed. Yet he was concerned. How long would this process take?

Keith's counselor thought it would take quite some time, but he believed there was good reason for hope in saving the relationship. Keith was angry, but he was also afraid of losing his family and his lifestyle. The question was how much he would do to preserve the life he loved and whether he would find it worth the cost. After considering a talk on the nature of change and growth, his counselor chose a different approach: "I wonder if you've noticed in the woods you hunt in, what happens when a tree grows?" he asked Keith. "Have you noticed that the way a tree grows affects all the other trees around it? It can crowd another tree and force it to bend. It can grow tall and overshadow the other, it can fall, destroying the other, or it can shift, making space for the other. But there is one thing it can't do. It can't change the basic nature of the other. An oak growing by a maple doesn't change the maple into an oak. The trees are always shifting, but they are directed by their own natures. Do you know what I mean?"

"You think I should shift," Keith said.

"Yes, and stay the same," his counselor said.

Keith tried again. "You think I can understand Joan better."

"Yes, and yourself and more than that," the counselor answered. "It could be a challenge."

Summary of Observations: ESTP

- A direct confrontation from his wife initiates a counseling contact for Keith, something that often occurs in the case of ESTP clients.

- Keith fears losing his relationship (and his leisure partner) to an inner journey that he does not understand or feel a part of.

- Keith wants (and needs) to be actively involved in the process of change.

- Keith can appeal to his ability to weigh the cost and consequences of a situation and to act on it.

- Keith needs encouragement to see that a paradox can be real.

Analysis: ESTP

Through the threatened dissolution of his marriage, Keith is presented with the opportunity for growth. It may be too much to expect him to immediately see it this way. He believes his task is to keep his marriage together, and, to his credit, he is attempting to do that—though it may be more difficult and time-consuming than simply showing up in a counseling office. His current anxiety provides him with an opportunity; it is doubtful that Keith would be drawn to contemplation about his relationship or his own growth potential without pressure of near-crisis proportions. And it may be unreasonable to expect him to enjoy the process or to welcome the pressure.

Before he and his wife can resolve their conflicts, he will need to recognize that the division between them has to do with him, as well as with his wife, and that it can only be resolved through interaction and internal shifting. Before the relationship can be healed, he will need to see that their conflict is not a black and white issue that can be reduced to a simple "I change" or "she changes" solution. Rather, it needs an approach that acknowledges their mutual involvement in the conflict. Since ambiguity is not something that Keith is comfortable with, this may be a struggle for him. He will also need to realize that he cannot "fix" his relationship and that there is nothing that he can do to resolve the problem from a distance. He must enter into it and devote time and energy to it without the benefit of knowing the outcome in advance, which is particularly difficult and frightening for him.

Keith's intelligence and ability to see things as they are—as well as his commitment to his marriage—may help him to understand the situation. He will need these assets, for he is not fully equipped to understand or tolerate Joan's new direction, which has probably always been an interest for her, but has been set aside in place of child-rearing responsibilities. His desire to avoid the pain of exploring conflict and his tendency to sum things up and then take action may be both helpful and problematic for him. He will deal with the pain and act when he knows what he must do—

but what is less clear is whether he can be patient enough to resist acting before he knows what he must do.

In typological terms, Keith needs to continue to be a lively, energetic, competent, fun-loving ESTP. In addition, the cultivation of some of his nonpreferred type preferences may help him understand and appreciate his wife, who is taking a new path. The cultivation of these nonpreferred preferences can also help him to become a more whole person. His introverted intuition, though largely unknown and primitive, can nevertheless bring depth to his understanding and anchor his knowing in the meaning of events, not just in the events themselves. For example, Joan's new path has meaning in that it threatens their valued relationship and leisure pursuits, both of which have a long history. It also has meaning in that Keith may realize and grow from recognizing his own limitations in understanding, tolerating, or changing this event. This will be difficult for him because introverted intuition surveys the inner landscape, moves at a slow pace, and is often inexact. Keith tends to survey the outer landscape, move at a quick pace, and desire precision. And though he will continue to favor this latter tendency, his current problem will not yield to outer, quick, and definitive action. His intuitive function may also help him come to realize that there are many ways of seeing things, most of which are gray rather than black or white. To deal with this less developed function, he will need to be open and slowly receptive to its indistinctive urgings and nudgings and to entertain and evaluate these clues, but not discount them because they seem unusual.

Keith's natural, strong, and practical sensing and thinking gifts may be his greatest helpers in this process. They may help him see the reasons for engaging in the process of counseling, as they help him see the benefits of working out the relationship and the consequences of not doing so. He is also likely to feel less resistant if he can honor the need of his sensing and thinking functions, as well as the need of his SP temperament, to actively participate in the process of working out a new way of living.

He will also need to develop his feeling function. His thinking function is working for him in that it tells him his family and lifestyle are at risk and that the consequences of inaction will be costly. His feeling function may help him not only realize that he may lose his family and lifestyle but also the meaning of losing them—how much he values them and how painful it would be for him to be without them. His feeling function may also, if he can develop it, help him to know what others value, letting him recognize and even appreciate differences in others—whether he understands them or not.

Keith's midlife task requires that he slow down and contemplate the possible meanings of changing relationships and lifestyles. He will move closer toward his center and feel more connected and receptive when he comes to recognize the limits of his problem-solving orientation and see the value of a multifaceted process, and when he comes to see the benefit of being able to travel through both the inner and outer landscapes.

Typological Descriptions: ESFP and ESTP

ESFP	ESTP
Open ear, open shoulder, open heart	*Negotiate, mediate, and get on with it*
Dominant extraverted sensing	Dominant extraverted sensing
Auxiliary introverted feeling	Auxiliary introverted thinking
Tertiary extraverted thinking	Tertiary extraverted feeling
Inferior introverted intuition	Inferior introverted intuition

Extraverted sensors focus their acute observational skills on collecting concrete data from the world around them, concentrating on what is, not on what has been or what might be. They need to see practical applications to real life in information. Gifted problem solvers, they focus on the moment, constantly scanning the environment and quickly sizing up any situation. They enjoy upbeat, high-energy environments. For them, the past is over and done with and the future is yet to come, so the focus stays on the present. Less likely to share their judgments, they offer their perceptions relating to the present moment.

ESFPs

ESFPs focus on relationships, scanning the environment for all data that relate to people. As catalysts, they focus on others, seeking harmony and a smooth, social atmosphere. They often hold back on constructive criticism due to their need to be liked and appreciated by others. Although they seek the input of others and prefer to have their agreement, they may still act according to their own internal values, thus presenting mixed messages to others. Believing that people are more important than organizations, they often feel responsible for cheering others up and being attentive to other people's needs. Under stress, they tend to make mountains out of molehills, believing something will go wrong, even if there is no evidence that it will. In midlife, recognizing the downside of always being cheerful and wanting everyone to like them may be helpful.

Just as it is with ESTPs, the SP temperament of ESFPs greatly impacts how they appear to and interact with their external environment. They have a playful sense of life, not taking it too seriously, focusing instead on the enjoyment of each moment. They bring a sense of fun and joie de vivre that tends to break down any barriers between their different personae. Living for the moment, they focus on the here-and-now, having little interest in either reviewing the past or making long-range plans for the future. They are frequently seen by others as procrastinators. Since they prefer "being out there and gathering information," they typically wait until the last minute to prepare intentionally for anything. Once they become excited by the challenge, they enjoy the spontaneity of being able to respond to whatever is presented at the moment. Unless their emotions and personal values become hooked, they are very adept and often stimulated by dealing with crisis situations.

They bring an insatiable need for action to any situation, having little patience with those who need to spend what they consider to be an exorbitant amount of time hashing and rehashing information and possible solutions to problems. Often irritated when others don't get to the point, they resist overanalyzing issues before taking action on them. Rules generally mean little to them, since they only reflect a past orientation. Rules are meant to be changed, just as traditions can be challenged when they no longer fit a present situation. They often see rules and traditions as guidelines to be followed when they are applicable and discarded when they seem inappropriate.

In the workplace, ESFPs prefer to be independent and be their own boss, which provides them with the freedom and flexibility they crave. However, they do seek an adequate amount of stimulation from people connections, so finding a balance between the two often becomes an important part of midlife for them. Thriving on newness and stimulation, they enjoy a frequent change of jobs. During midlife, the intuitive and thinking functions of ESFPs seem increasingly compelling and available to them.

Their inferior introverted intuition also tends to assert itself at midlife. They often find it difficult to grasp and very unappealing, frequently viewing intuitives as giving the impression of being superior and very learned while actually being not grounded in the reality of the present moment. When they are under stress, their inferior function can suddenly and unexpectedly appear, causing them to exaggerate the difficulties of a situation, in sharp contrast to their usual easygoing, laid-back style. They may then become convinced that everything is going wrong, even when there is no evidence to support this conclusion.

By learning to honor their inner feeling function, they can briefly stop "maneuvering" out there and learn to maneuver inside, recognizing their need for occasional inner focus. Becoming increasingly aware of and loyal to their own values and goals is often an important step in focusing their lives. Their inferior intuition may eventually help them become increasingly aware of patterns in their lives—both positive and negative— connections between things that have happened to them and how they fit together. In a crisis, they may make snap decisions which they regret later after time for reflection. With increasing awareness, they learn to make more conscious choices regarding important decisions.

Their thinking function can help increase their awareness of the consequences of their actions, especially as they relate to their impact on others. They tend to have difficulty being objective, since they may be influenced by their own values and relationships. Considering such questions as "So what?" and "What difference will this information make?" may help them analyze the pros and cons and alternative ways of behaving and interacting with others. A more intentional thinking-judging focus at midlife may help them concentrate more on the completion of a task when necessary by developing increased comfort with some organizational and planning skills. By learning how to put all the pieces together, they may gain a clearer picture of the patterns in their lives.

In midlife, ESFPs talk about needing to focus more so they can avoid overextending themselves on a regular basis. Tied to this is the necessity of continuing to honor their need for stimulation, fun, excitement, and spontaneity.

ESTPs

In contrast, ESTPs are stimulated by problem-solving and crisis situations and are increasingly energized by the need for action. They do not hesitate to modify or bend the rules to adapt to the current situation, making whatever changes are necessary. However, because they tend to resist organizational structures, they may solve the same problem over and over again. They need freedom to move in their own directions, to do something different every day. As practical decision makers, they use down-to-earth considerations along with a sense of urgency. With a flare for the dramatic, they exude a sense of enthusiasm and of fun—an experiential enjoyment of life, of living life to the fullest.

At midlife, they learn to examine more fully the value of other people's new ideas, which often seem weird to them, before they evaluate and discard them. Since they prefer to focus on their external world, they may expend energy on ideas that are not well thought out, thus indicating their need for sufficient introverted time to access their inner thinking. Increased attention to their inferior inner intuition may eventually help them identify patterns and connections in their experiences so that they

84

can understand them more fully. They tend to have little compassion with complainers, exhorting them to "fix it or stop complaining." Focusing on objective reality, they don't easily trust abstract theories or concepts, preferring realistic ideas and practical ways to apply them in a present situation. Their "feeling," which is often translated through their thinking preference, is used more often to pick up external cultural values than it is to become aware of and more sensitive to other people's feelings.

More likely to express their feelings regarding external events, ESTPs are less likely to communicate their inner struggles. When they decide to do so, they need others to be warm, supportive, and patient. They have a tendency to make abrupt decisions that may later require reevaluation. Often they become stuck with their hurt feelings, unable to find a way out, even though logically they understand what they need to do. At midlife, they are increasingly able to recognize when they experience certain emotions. Learning to label their feelings may be an important first step toward communicating their emotions to others.

The Midlife Transition: ESFP and ESTP

Extraverted Sensing Style: Journey Is a Funny Word

ESFP

Now is the time.

ESTP

If it's important, do it.

Characteristics of ESFPs and ESTPs

- Too much activity and too little satisfaction
- Desire to get some control over life
- Optimism—even in the face of pain
- A high tolerance for stress and an ability to change if change seems desirable
- Orientation toward changing outer reality rather than inner reality

Particularly True for ESFPs

A need for fun, surprises, and lighthearted activities

Particularly True for ESTPs

A need for spontaneity and precise, directed activity

Relationship Issues

Other people (depending partially on their own type preferences) may

- Perceive them as nonreflective and unable/unwilling to look at the meaning of events, as well as the events themselves, and to experience inner reality as well as outer reality
- Perceive them as one-track and unable/unwilling to look at alternatives, especially ones that don't make sense to them
- Perceive them as avoiding pain and lacking patience

Others should try to

- Understand their own needs and biases and be empathetic to the person's resistance to introspection, slow pace, and lack of clarity
- Appear optimistic and competent and maintain an active, quick-paced process that can hold the person's interest

ESFP   ESTP

Particularly with ESFPs, others should	*Particularly with ESTPs, others should*
Affirm them by appreciating their charm and presentness and offering them a concrete, direct approach	Honor them by appreciating their reality orientation and willingness to act and offer direct challenge when needed

Guidelines for Helping ESFPs and ESTPs Through Midlife

Recognize and confirm the strengths of extraverted sensors—their keen observation skills, ability to be concrete, to be aware of and live in present, ordinary reality, and to know when to act

Particularly with ESFPs, others should try to confirm their	*Particularly with ESTPs, others should try to confirm their*
Ability to affirm and relate warmly to others and to take action	Ability to make tough decisions and act under pressure

Encourage balance to extraverted sensors (which will also help them develop their intuitive skills) by

- Encouraging a broader vision—expanding options and opening categories that are too small

- Encouraging them to let go of their tendency to discount what is not concrete and clear—or what requires sustained investigation

- Encouraging appreciation of many ways of knowing, including hunches, dreams, and fantasies

- Honoring a sense of internal as well as external life

- Encouraging connection of different realities to the past, the present, and especially the future

Particularly Helpful for ESFPs	*Particularly Helpful for ESTPs*
Encourage close attention to the consequences of one's actions	Encourage close attention to what matters to oneself and to others

Profile: INFJ

Sandra was an attractive 48-year-old woman. She clearly took great care with her appearance and the way she presented herself. Her mixture of reserve and warmth were intriguing. She often spoke of her family, her interest in art, and her job as an employee recruiter for a large medical practice. She sometimes spoke of her interest in meditation, dream work, and her love of nature. At work, she was responsible for hiring and training all new employees for a multi-city medical firm, and she enjoyed both her work and her family. It was obvious that something was bothering Sandra, though she had difficulty talking about it. It seemed that she needed to tell her story, as difficult as that might be, and have it heard.

One day while talking to a close and trusted friend, Sandra began to describe the confusion in her life. "I need someone to help me sort out my confusion," she began. "Something important is missing in my life. There has got to be more to life than what I've found. This is hard to talk about. I'm not sure I can make you understand. I've got so many obligations; I need some time for myself. I like to paint, and I haven't had a brush in my hands for two years—that's crazy. But I don't have time. It takes all I've got to stay on top of my job and my family. I'm always behind. There are twenty books on the shelf in my office that I should have read but haven't."

Her friend wondered why Sandra felt she had to read all the books. Sandra explained that she believed she would be able to do her job better if she had read, and digested, all of them. Sandra wasn't sure she could prepare anything she had not thoroughly studied and rehearsed, and she couldn't bear for people not to be pleased with her. She remembered a seminar she had conducted for some new employees at her firm. The evaluations were good in general, but two people had complained. Only two out of forty people were displeased, but still she worried about it. Sandra realized she wasn't being rational, but she still couldn't forget about it. She believed that if she had been better prepared, all of the participants would have been pleased. She could laugh at the way she felt about this, but only a little.

"I do need to be prepared," she explained. "It would be stressful and risky for me to try to make myself understood without being prepared, but I don't want my need for preparation and for doing everything right to block my work and my joy...to keep me feeling overextended and tired and unable to paint and to do the other things that I want. Not having people understand and appreciate me is a big problem, and now it's taking up too much time and energy. I've just recently become aware of how unhappy I am sometimes in my work, and that is when my boss doesn't support me."

"What does support mean?" her friend wondered aloud.

"It means he doesn't listen to me. He doesn't support me when he doesn't speak up for me in the management committee and when he doesn't give me feedback until he has something negative to say. He doesn't seem to care much about me—only about what I do."

Her friend agreed that it would be nice if people were more caring and there were less conflict in Sandra's life, but she wondered how realistic that was. And she wondered why Sandra didn't see that it was unrealistic. She thought it might be more helpful for Sandra to learn how to face conflict and work through it, but she was afraid to tell her that.

There was a period of silence. Sandra sounded a bit annoyed as she said, "I know I shouldn't worry so much about conflict, that I should face unpleasantness, but I don't want to. That's the way I am." It sounded like a closed subject to her friend.

Yet Sandra wished for a minute that she could imagine what it would be like if "they" didn't matter so much and if she didn't care so much about what they thought. She wondered when she might find what made her happiest and most productive.

As she reflected, she realized that her happiest moments were when she had time to dream, think, and meditate. She was happy when she had a few people who could understand what she had to say and who would listen to her and help her sort things out and care for her. She realized that her need for perfection and external approval was costing her what she most wanted and needed at this stage of her life.

Sandra knew she had a lot to say and might have a great deal more to say, if only she took the time to contemplate. She also knew that she had difficulty putting her thoughts into words that people could understand. She wondered if she could learn how to not feel so judged by people who weren't interested in or perhaps had no need for what she had to offer. She knew judgment was a big problem for her, not only because it was painful but also because it might block her creativity and her path.

"That word judgment gives me a chill," she said to her friend. "I grew up feeling I was always being judged. My family does it now. And I've stopped going to church. It is all about a judging God—a God out there somewhere. I'm not interested in talking about God out there—out there who knows where. I want to bring forth what's in me."

"It's so important," she continued. "I couldn't bear to have it rejected." Her friend wondered what "it" was.

Summary of Observations: INFJ

- Sandra needs to tell her life story—and have it heard—in order to understand it.

- Sandra has difficulty expressing her perceptions to others.

- Sandra's perfectionistic tendencies are her defense against criticism and conflict.

- Sandra thinks preparation is necessary but also realizes the cost of doing too much of it.

- Sandra has difficulty working with people who don't support and affirm her.

- Sandra needs to avoid shouldering all the blame for her problems, but she also needs to take some responsibility for facing conflict and working through disagreements.

- Sandra needs to find relief from external demands in order to devote some time to her special gifts—deep reflection and creativity.

- Sandra has the ability to reach a deep, personal, and spiritual place within herself.

Analysis: INFJ

Sandra is facing a midlife vocational issue. Problems with vocational issues often appear as seething discontent that lies just below a calm, collected surface. Sandra must bring forth what is in her—whether this be her creativity, her inclination to learn and teach others, her spirituality, or other things. But she is stifled and complains of not having time to prepare for her work. Thus, she feels a loss of control. She thinks that if she is "good enough"—that is, if she can compensate for her feelings of inadequacy by being prepared—she can protect herself from the judgment and criticism of others. She hopes that if she is good enough that people will affirm her, and she is paralyzed by fear of what she sees as rejection. This rejection is particularly terrible, since she sees it not just as rejection of her work but of herself. Yet she knows she has something important to give—in fact, she has something she must give—and this knowledge will cause her to grow, as painful as that may be.

She thinks she needs time, and she is right. She needs time to dream, to paint, and to be in touch with what is within her. She has a depth and a sensitivity that both she and the world can benefit from. She needs to be a bit more realistic about how much acceptance one can reasonably expect from other people, and she needs to learn to present her ideas with conviction and flexibility.

In typological terms, Sandra (as is the case with most introverted intuitives) needs to pay attention to her greatest gift—introverted intuition—with its ability to allow her to reach depths and see patterns so that she can learn what many other people don't know, and to learn how to see things differently from the way her outer world sees them. She needs time and space and to honor introverted intuitive ways of knowing, such as meditation and contemplation, and she needs to validate the subtle nudging she receives from her unconscious. She feels overextended and short of time, but the time she needs should focus primarily on her inner world, not her outer world.

Her gifted extraverted feeling, which is what she meets the world with, is, in this case, also her adversary. Its relational quality leaves her constantly occupied with pleasing others and meeting their expectations. This extraverted feeling relational quality and the need to be accepted can be harmful to all NFs, but is particularly troublesome for introverted intuitives with a feeling preference. Sandra's feeling orientation seeks approval, and when introverted intuition is communicated, often inadequately, it may be met with rejection rather than approval. The rejection is then taken personally and generalized. If what she offers other people is not received, she may feel that she herself is not received.

In her need to please others and communicate with other people, Sandra has honored her extraverted feeling at the expense of her greatest gift—introverted intuition. She needs to stop usurping her dominant intuition with its helpmate, feeling. Her thinking function can help her in this undertaking because it can bring some understanding and objectivity to the process. It may help her to see that a rejection of her ideas is not necessarily a rejection of her. It may help her realize that some people can't—or won't—hear her, and this can help her evaluate the cost of letting her life be determined from the outside rather than the inside. It may also help her cope with conflict, convincingly communicate her ideas, and adjust her ideas when it makes sense to do so. It may help her understand her responsibility, as well as her ability, to work through conflict.

If she looks within herself, she may also find that she not only has extraverted feeling but also introverted feeling. She can determine what matters to herself as well as to other people. If she can touch her core values, they may help her find the strength to face a world that is not always friendly or accepting. It may also help her let go of some things that don't meet her values, freeing up some much needed time for such personal activities as reflection, dreaming, and painting.

Her extraverted sensing, though basically unexplored and undervalued, can also help her to accept an imperfect world with its mundaneness. Like most intuitives, she has a life task to "make things real." Her sensing function has a gift for making things real. It can help her accept things as they are, rather than as they might be, and it can encourage her to "do" as well as "dream." With some luck, her sensing function might even produce a connection with her body, with nature, and with her sensuality, all of which can ground Sandra and offer her not only movement toward wholeness but also great joy.

Sandra's midlife task requires that she establish boundaries and give up overreliance on the approval of others. She will be closer to her center and feel less caged, stretched, afraid, misunderstood, and inadequate and more relaxed, flowing, and connected to her inner self and to others when she can believe in herself, give up some of her need for affirmation and perfection, and trust her inner values and vision.

Profile: INTJ

Raoul, a tall dignified man with a slightly aloof manner, had been briefly hospitalized for stress and exhaustion the previous year. He now feels that he must get his life back on track and set some goals. While his recovery was unusually rapid, he had been in significant psychological difficulty. One night, Raoul found that he simply couldn't remember anything. He couldn't remember what had gone on at work that day, and he couldn't remember what he was to do the next day. He spent the weekend in the hospital, and then that critical period passed. After seeing a psychiatrist for a year, Raoul thought he was almost back to normal, but the breakdown was really embarrassing for him. He thought he should have been able to handle himself better. He acknowledged the fact that at the time of his illness he had been under a lot of stress at work and that his son had a serious drug problem, but he reasoned that he should have been able to manage. Raoul believed that his stress was primarily work related. The previous year work had been especially hard for him. His company was in a poor market and Raoul had been required to do things he felt uncomfortable with. He felt that he was selling out. Actually, he didn't just feel uncomfortable with his actions, he felt that he had been dishonest and blamed himself for not standing up for himself and refusing to participate in what he felt were shady deals. He didn't like himself for becoming involved with some of the things that were going on at his company.

Raoul's self-blame was painful for those around him. He was articulate and bright, appeared very deliberate, and didn't offer words lightly. In fact, he didn't like to discuss his personal situation with others, and when he did it was because he was convinced it would help him get on with his life. It took strength for him to admit a weakness.

During his illness, Raoul was unable do his work, so his staff worked hard and held things together. They had "picked up the ball and carried it," as he put it. He did not like putting them in that position, nor did he like finding himself in a position where he had to be cared for. After all, Raoul thought that it was his role to lead them. He didn't like weak people or people who played the part of "the hurt one." Raoul was surprised to realize what he was slowly becoming aware of—he knew exactly what he was learning and struggled to find some way to express the nebulous material he was beginning to touch but still did not trust.

Raoul tried to confide this to his wife one evening. "I learned that I can be with people who are sick and not believe they are weak. I never felt that before. I often thought if people were sick, it might somehow be their fault—perhaps if they didn't take care of themselves or eat correctly. But last week, when you were sick, I felt really bad for you."

Raoul and his wife were both glad to receive this new awareness, but Raoul was most concerned about what he was to do next. "I feel undirected—like I'm floating and don't know where I fit. I don't know how to be me and how to live my life. I'm not sure I want to stay in my job. How can I work so hard at something I don't believe in? My work requires too many hours, but what can I do? My staff was great when I was sick, but I really can't rely on them to stay with things and do them right. I have to check on them all the time. And I'm relieved that our son's off drugs now and in the treatment program—but he's never stuck to anything before, so I don't know that he is going to stick to this. I don't see why he doesn't see what he has to do and just do it. I don't understand him. I need to decide how to deal with him and my staff, too."

It all felt questionable to Raoul. It was hard for him to sort out what he could understand and deal with from what he couldn't, and it was hard for him to separate his responsibilities from those of others.

Raoul's wife sensed his discomfort when he talked about feeling responsible for holding other people to his standards, his fear of inauthenticity and vulnerability, and his discomfort with not having clear goals. She sensed his tension and wondered why he thought he had to push the biggest rock up the hill all alone.

"How does it feel to have to set the world straight?" she asked him.

"Like I would be irresponsible if I didn't," he responded, almost without hesitation. She heard his response, but she thought she had clearly asked how he *felt*.

She tried again. "How do you feel when you talk of being irresponsible?" Raoul gave no reply. "Does your back hurt? Are your shoulders stiff? Does your head hurt?" she prompted.

"Yes," he said. "I get a headache, especially at the temples. That happens when I get into this kind of conversation." She told him that she thought he was entitled to have a crummy feeling or two once in awhile.

Raoul couldn't respond to this, but he suddenly remembered a dream that he wanted to share with his wife. "You know," he said. "I had this interesting dream last night. Would you like to hear it?"

Summary of Observations: INTJ

- Raoul blames himself and judges himself harshly.
- Raoul has a strong need for inner and outer authenticity and integrity.
- Raoul will work diligently for any outcome he deems worthy of effort.
- Raoul has difficulty trusting and articulating his deep, nebulous insights.

- Raoul recognizes the correlation between his tendency to be judgmental of weaknesses in himself and in others.

- Raoul needs to recognize his limitations and his vulnerabilities.

- For Raoul, conceptualization and evaluation are natural, but he needs to learn how to know and express deep inner emotions as well.

- For Raoul, some awareness of his body sensations and deep emotions, as well as his thoughts, can help him come to know what things are really important to him.

- The world of dreams and imagination might offer Raoul real, rich data, which his willpower and cognition can't provide.

Analysis: INTJ

Raoul's emotional illness devastated him briefly by removing his sense of control and competency. It challenged his ability to understand himself, and it leaves him blaming himself for his weakness. It also introduces something that Raoul needs to know more about in himself and in others—vulnerability and weakness. Raoul already understands vulnerability, for he can now be with a person who is ill and not immediately conclude that the person is weak. Raoul, precisely because of his awareness of his own weakness, is more related and compassionate. He has not, however, generalized the empathy he feels for people suffering from illness to other areas of life. Raoul still believes he must bear all the weight of work and family problems. He thinks that he must be strong, that he must understand, and that he must find solutions to all problems. He has a lot to learn about his own limitations.

On one hand, Raoul's commitment to understanding, managing, and improving his outer world is genuine and honorable, and he needs to manage and improve all he can. He often demonstrates integrity in dealing with the outer world, and his extraverted thinking function is a great asset here. One might wonder about his commitment to the integrity of his inner world—that place of personal vision and truth that appears to be neglected and which his dominant introverted intuition could lead him to if it were honored. In fact, the conflict brought about by Raoul acting in a way incongruent with his inner truth (neglecting his dominant type preference) in favor of his auxiliary contributed to his illness.

To honor his inner world, the place that houses his creative core, Raoul will have to find time and space for inner exploration. This will require him to reduce the amount of energy spent on setting and administering standards for others and may leave him feeling as if he is shortchanging his responsibilities. Many people need to be concerned about being accountable, but Raoul takes on an abundance of responsibility. And while he must hold onto these traits, he should also make room for other parts of himself.

His growth areas at midlife center around discovering and honoring his own personal emotional being, accepting his vulnerability and inability to understand and piece together neatly everything that is happening to him. His depth of vision, his ability to make connections, his ability to change, and his core creativity can lead him through this period.

In typological terms, Raoul needs to relax his extraverted thinking and let his other typological functions bring some sense of balance to his life. His extraverted thinking has been invaluable to him in his work as a manager, in his role as primary wage-earner in the family, and as a male in American society. It has helped him understand life, formulate goals, establish codes of conduct, adhere to general principles, explain his positions, and move ahead in a linear, logical, and efficient way. It's not surprising that extraverted thinking is in control of his life, but it has also created problems, since Raoul is a dominant introverted intuitive and not a dominant thinker. Introverted intuition operates from a very different place than does extraverted thinking. It often sees many sides of the same issue, denies pure rationality, is nonlinear, and is difficult to communicate. At the same time, it can offer Raoul flexibility, depth, creativity, and renewal.

Raoul doesn't recognize this. He thinks he wants to return to what he knows—his extraverted thinking world—so he can fit into his work and be comforted by goals and a sense of control. But he can't, since that is the world that made him ill. When he puts his dominant introverted intuition back in the driver's seat, he may find that his dreams, just as much as his analysis, give his life guidance and help him establish goals and strategies. If he can honor his introverted intuition, he may learn to let go of some judgment, wait for resolutions to emerge from within, and come to see the many sides of most issues. But most important, he may come to know his own individual and personal truth in addition to the truth of external rules, laws, and principles. And in this knowing, he may discover that he has a sense of deeper integrity that revitalizes his life, especially as his well-developed extraverted thinking helps him place his own special truth in the world. He will find new goals that are connected to his self, not just his ego.

His feeling and sensing functions can also help. His feeling function can tell him what he values and what others value, without the influence of what he projects onto them. In doing so, his feeling function can bring balance to the objective and nonpersonal nature of extraverted thinking. He may even find that he wants relationships with his son and staff members as much as he wants them to behave in a prescribed manner.

His sensing, if he can recognize its subtle nuances, can ground him in the present moment and help him realize that, while goals and a future direction are important, he lives in the present. The act of planting a garden may come to be as important as the future harvest. His sensing may also help him to see that things are the way they are, and not necessarily as he wishes or imagines them to be. It may help him to learn how to live with imperfections, even though he won't like it. His sensing may even bring him joy as it teaches him about sensuality through such things as the taste of good food, the relaxed feel of a body after exercise or sexual activity, or the joy of a new flower blooming in his garden.

Raoul's midlife task requires that he shift his emphasis from goals, objectives, and standards to recognizing, trusting, and using his authentic personal truth as a guide for action. He will be closer to his center and feel more playful, creative, authentic and less judgmental and driven when he recognizes the limitations of a general, logical, linear, problem-solving approach to the world and is able to access his own personal, subjective way of knowing and valuing as a guide for action. He will feel less defensive and more connected to others when he can accept appropriate vulnerability.

Typological Descriptions: INFJ and INTJ

INFJ	INTJ
Searching for the melody of life	*Our eyes perceive no boundaries*
Dominant introverted intuition	Dominant introverted intuition
Auxiliary extraverted feeling	Auxiliary extraverted thinking
Tertiary introverted thinking	Tertiary introverted feeling
Inferior extraverted sensing	Inferior extraverted sensing

Although INFJs and INTJs have the same dominant function, they tend to lead with their extraverted auxiliaries—either feeling or thinking—and therefore may appear very different.

For many INTJs and INFJs, however, midlife is a time for learning to trust their dominant intuition, which has often seemed nebulous and unfocused. Introverted intuitives make quick internal connections, often entering conversations at whatever point they decide to present their ideas—ideas that may be totally unrelated to anything else in the conversation. Jung described the way dominant introverted intuitives often put their ideas into the outer world, only to recognize that others often don't understand them. This may then cause them to retreat inward and internally censor their ideas before they share them with others. This process may lead to great inner intensity. Taking sufficient time to internalize their intuitive process before sharing their ideas might help them to see patterns and recognize relationships. Learning to trust their introverted intuition, therefore, necessitates first learning to validate it for themselves.

For both types, extraverted sensing, their inferior function, can create problems for them when they feel overwhelmed by details. When under stress, they may become almost immobilized, as they attempt to make sense of large amounts of seemingly unrelated data. Guided by an energizing intuition that can lead them in too many directions, they may become increasingly overwhelmed and frustrated with unrelated material. Use of their judging preference—either thinking or feeling—to choose and focus may help them sort through data and become less fragmented and more centered again.

Both thinkers and feelers in general tend to ignore physical data, frequently failing to recognize physical stress symptoms until they seem to suddenly reach crisis proportions. Keeping busy, with almost frantic motions—a common way for them to deal with stress—may postpone their identification of the causes of their stress, even to the point that they deny that it exists. Becoming more intentional about learning to identify early symptoms of stress may encourage them to break from the task, finding ways to alleviate the stress through exercise, meditation, or other energizing activities. Slowing down the pace of life and living more fully in the present can also help them reduce their stress by increasing their awareness of the internal and external triggers that tend to cause it.

For both types, sensing can also become a means of enjoying nature, enabling them to focus on the moment and the wonders of creation. By increasing their awareness of the beauty of the natural world around them, they may feel more grounded and connected to nature—listening to, experiencing, and seeing a whole new world. Many INJs talk about how they enjoy taking up new artistic pursuits, crafts, or other creative hobbies at midlife as a way of "seeing" the world around them through different lenses. However they choose to incorporate their inferior sensing, the act of doing so may help them feel centered and more in tune with their inner intuition.

INFJs

For INFJs, extraverting their feeling preference involves focusing on people and interacting with them. Through supporting others, listening, and being available to them, INFJs build relationships with both individuals and groups. Their tendency to want to please others stems from their feeling function and prompts them to be good listeners who value being empathic to others' needs, often at the expense of their own. Since they find disharmony painful and even debilitating, they may tend to give in to others in order to avoid conflict, often accepting blame for failure in relationships. Owning, valuing, and communicating their emotional needs is often difficult for them, but important at midlife, as they come to recognize that the frequent intensity they project when they are grasping for inner connections and understanding can alienate others. Telling their stories and believing they are being heard can help them clarify, make connections, and validate their own inner experiences. They can then begin to recognize that the answers they seek are within themselves.

Learning to trust their experience, seek inner validation, and recognize that the answers they seek are within them are important steps toward trusting dominant intuition. Objective thinking can help them become increasingly comfortable with conflict and differences of opinion. Becoming more assertive about their own needs may enable them to let go of some of their "pleasing persona," helping them to recognize that achieving harmony is not solely their responsibility. They may then move toward being able to speak more confidently on issues of concern to them and articulate their values with increased clarity, logic, and objectivity.

For INFJs, coming to trust their dominant intuition is a critical step toward using the thinking function to accept conflict and differences of opinion. Their thinking function can help them speak out more confidently on issues of concern to them and articulate their values more logically and objectively.

At midlife, with some pain and struggle, INFJs often learn to express their own feelings and values more openly, thus validating their own strengths as well as honoring the differences they find in others. Trusting their own instincts often promotes increased self-acceptance. As they learn not to shoulder all the blame for conflicts that occur in their relationships, they also become more open to the necessary struggles that are often required to work through disagreements. Recognizing that, as one INFJ put it, "cultural expectations have inhibited our quest for identity," they now move into the second half of life, gaining increased clarity of who they are, validating their own sense of uniqueness and the ultimate questions they have about themselves and the world.

INTJs

During the first part of their lives, thinking controls most everything for INTJs, as they tend to define themselves predominantly through their work personae and what they do. Constantly conceptualizing and critiquing, they judge both themselves and others against the high standards of perfection they set for themselves. As a strongly independent type, being in charge enables INTJs to have sufficient independence, a necessary element since they tend to resist modifying their ideas or behavior to fit the job or system.

During midlife, the auxiliary thinking preference of INTJs continues its role of power, especially in the external world. Because of their great need for competence in everything they do, INTJs can often be their own worst critics when they've made a mistake. Becoming grounded again in their dominant intuition may help them consider other options and new directions.

Increased attention to their dominant intuition enables INTJs to trust it more fully, to listen to it, and to follow where it leads them. "How does this all fit together? What do I really want to spend my life doing? What is the meaning of this for me?" Asking such questions emphasizes the need for inner and outer congruence, both of which are important issues for INTJs. Attention and affirmation of their dominant intuition also gives them increased confidence in their own perceptions and acceptance of their strengths without reservations.

Developing their feeling preference seems to focus primarily on three areas: recognizing and articulating their own emotions and feelings, clarifying their personal values, and reaching out more to others in relationships. During the first half of life, their sense of independence often provides an objective shield for them in the area of relationships, making it difficult for them to recognize and express how they feel. One INTJ said, "I don't put who I am out to other people. If someone says, 'I don't know you,' I take that as a compliment." However, midlife seems to draw INTJs further into the personal arena—selectively and slowly, but with increasing interest and desire. As they become more aware of their emotions, they may allow themselves to experience them and name them, to "own" them as a part of themselves, and eventually decide to express them more consciously and freely.

INTJs place a high value on independence reflected in a sense of inner and outer congruence. In midlife, they often bring increased clarity to their own value systems, evaluating their congruence with external and institutional values. Where there are differences, they may not support the people, systems, and organizations that do not fit their own values.

The Midlife Transition: INFJ and INTJ

Introverted Intuitive Style: Plunge the Depths

INFJ

The journey is about getting out of the shell.

INTJ

This isn't a quest. It's how I and the big plan fit.

Characteristics of INFJs and INTJs

- Inner intensity that is unexpressed
- Realization that inner and outer lives are incongruent
- A connection to unconscious materials
- Vague discontent
- Interest in ultimate questions

Particularly True for INFJs

Need affirmation and encouragement

Particularly True for INTJs

Need comprehension and direction

Relationship Issues

Other people (depending partially on their own type preferences) may

- Experience them as having difficulty entrusting their personal thoughts, feelings, and beliefs to anyone
- Recognize a hidden sadness or even anger in them for not being accepted for who they are
- Experience them as blaming of themselves and/or others

Others should try to

- Understand their own needs and biases and be empathetic to the person's resistance to simplistic, surface explanations and distrust of other people's ability to understand

Particularly with INFJs, others should	*Particularly with INTJs, others should*
Affirm and validate them and patiently listen to them and honor their fear of disharmony	Respect their tendency to search for their core truth and honor their fear of vulnerability

Guidelines for Helping INFJs and INTJs Through Midlife

Recognize and confirm the strengths of introverted intuitives—their vision, intensity, depth, individuality, sense of responsibility, and determination

Particularly with INFJs, others should try to confirm their	*Particularly with INTJs, others should try to confirm their*
Ability to empathize with others	Ability to search for their own truth and hold onto it in the face of opposition

Encourage balance to introverted intuitives (which will also help them develop their sensing skills) by

- Encouraging them to connect to "everydayness" and concrete reality
- Encouraging them to be aware of their body and what it can teach them—integrate the body/mind split
- Encouraging them to act in the world
- Encouraging them to make concrete, focused communication
- Encouraging them to spend introverted time honoring their dominant introverted intuition

Particularly Helpful for INFJs	*Particularly Helpful for INTJs*
Encourage less personalizing and generalizing of negative feedback	Encourage them to give up blame and honor relatedness and appropriate vulnerability

Profile: ENFP

Terrance made people feel comfortable and affirmed when in his presence. He was a good listener and conveyed empathy, often nodding in understanding as people spoke to him. Terrance was a Protestant minister who now found himself in a quandary. He had decided to leave the ministry and look for a different line of work.

"I do feel called to the ministry," he said, "but the church is such a boring bureaucracy, and I've had it with bureaucracy. It's also more than just bureaucracy and boredom—it's worse than that. I think of the church as being in the "meaning business," and it feels like nothing I do has any meaning. Most of my church's leaders want a commander—a good administrator. I could spend all my time doing that, but I don't want to."

Terrance was right. His congregation did think he was disorganized, overcommitted, and fragmented—but they were generally fond of him anyway. Terrance talked with a career counselor about his desire to change his career.

"I have a friend," he told the counselor, "who is directing a conference center in Maine, and I envy him. Every day is different for him, and he is doing important work. They have interesting people bring exciting programs there all the time. Last year he told me that he organized a conference with world-known leaders to look at an emerging cosmology for the twenty-first century. And many of their lectures and workshops draw hundreds of people who come from all parts of the country. I can't see that happening in my church."

His counselor asked Terrance if he were thinking of conference work for himself. Terrance didn't know, though he thought it sounded appealing. What he did know was that he wanted out of his church. He wanted to leave it soon—move to a new place and start over in a new field. He felt that both he and his family needed a change. The counselor asked Terrance about his family.

"There's a problem there," Terrance said. After hesitating, he continued. "I got involved with a woman about a year ago. I really didn't mean to. Life was dull, she was exciting and interesting, and she needed my help.

I am good at helping people who are having difficulty, and I felt good about helping her. In any case, her life seemed to be falling apart and I got hooked. In the process, I hurt my wife and my children—and my church. I regret that."

Terrance did feel regretful for his actions. He cared about people and wanted to be approved by them. One of Terrance's strongest gifts was his ability to care for and make a connection with others. He didn't want to hurt people who were important to him.

It was hard for Terrance to talk about the harmful consequences of his actions, but he was very perceptive. After months of exploration, he told his counselor, "I really didn't think a great deal about any of this at the time. During that period, it was as though I were on automatic pilot. I would give anything to repair the damage, but I can't. Now I need to move on and start over. We all need to start over."

Terrance had no shortage of ideas about how he should start over, but it was difficult to identify a personal connection to any one of them. Which one should he follow? Terrance didn't know. He really wanted to pursue all of them. He had trouble eliminating options. He had trouble saying no to people and he also had difficulty rejecting ideas. They were all good in his mind. How was he to know?

His counselor suggested he start by paying attention to his energy level, by monitoring what made him excited and brought him joy as well as what he did simply because it was required or just because it would please others. He was to write the special, joyful moments he experienced and bring his account of them to his next counseling session. His counselor suggested he pay attention to his body and asked how his body responded when he experienced boredom. Did he get sleepy, did his mind drift, did he feel physically heavy? Was it possible for him to learn something from the boredom and meaninglessness he found in bureaucracy? Terrance said he hadn't thought much about such things. His counselor wondered if Terrance's life might feel meaningless to him because he was not using his gifts. His homework task was to imagine his work with less bureaucracy and how he would spend his newly freed-up time. He was then to bring written scenarios of how he would do this to his next session.

"Find your inner voice," his counselor finally told him. Terrance worried about self-centeredness, selfishness, and the isolated nature of inner voices, but he agreed to give it a try. For Terrance, life was more about belonging than inner voices.

"I guess I need an action plan," he joked to himself, knowing that what he really needed was to focus on his next step and his commitment to follow through on it.

Summary of Observations: ENFP

- Terrance has the ability to make others feel affirmed and accepted in his presence.

- Terrance finds ordinariness and lack of meaning frustrating; he seeks excitement and a sense of purpose.

- Terrance was swayed by his feelings at a particular moment and failed to weigh the potential consequences of his actions.

- Terrance's imagination and expansiveness work for and against him.

- Terrance often sacrifices his innermost needs to the needs of others and to the requirements of the outside world.

- It will be more effective for Terrance to take small concrete steps and make commitments that are more realistic and demanding than it will be for him to make long-range abstract plans.

Analysis: ENFP

Terrance's extramarital affair and his frustration with bureaucracy force him to look at his way of operating, which is marked by openness, an enthusiasm for life, expansiveness, and action untempered by much inner reflection or sense of meaning and purpose.

This difficult situation forces him to look at the pain that he has brought on others and some of his own unexplored darkness. He cannot just brush the problem aside. There is no way in this situation that he can set everything right, make everyone happy and comfortable, and not see himself as responsible for the pain he has caused. His immediate response, as is typical for him in the face of serious conflict, is to try to wipe the slate clean and start anew. Yet, to his credit, this time he decides to take some time to reflect on his course of action. Feeling as badly as he does, he has the opportunity to learn to live with and accept flawed, everyday, and often boring reality. He has the opportunity to learn the price of responding to situations without regard for the potential consequences of his actions. He has the opportunity to see the price he will pay— namely boredom and meaninglessness—for not using his primary gifts and being cut off from his inner world.

In typological terms, his well-developed intuition can offer him enthusiasm, hope, and options, while his feeling function can offer him the ability to understand others and connect with them. He needs to devote some attention to his introverted feeling function in order to balance the outer direction of extraverted intuition and his intuitive feeling temperament. Introverted feeling can help him discover how he connects to his own personal, deeply held values as well as the values of those around him.

If he can develop it, his thinking function might help him see the potential consequences and outcomes of his actions, both to himself and to others. With a slower pace, he might be able to access his thinking function in the moment before he acts without thinking. His thinking function can perhaps also help him come to realize that he can't please everyone and that he can live without their approval. It might grant him some personal objectivity and help him to realize that although he does have a dark unexplored side, he himself is not that dark side. And while he may feel like an unfaithful person, he needs to realize that he is also a good person.

His sensing function, though underdeveloped, unknown, and primitive, can help him focus on and stay grounded in ordinariness and in the present. It might help him appreciate what he perceives as mundane situations or mundane people. He may even come to appreciate some of the bureaucracy he faces in his work. Some development of his SJ temperament could also provide him with discipline, focus, and follow-through. In small doses, his sensing, and his introverted sensing in particular, might help him to remain with situations—to mull them over and take them inside himself rather than defend against them by hopping quickly to different situations. His life might even be enriched by his sensing if he can take the time to appreciate nature and to care for his body and his surroundings.

Terrance's midlife task requires that he recognize his need for reflection, his inability to respond to everyone's wishes, and the necessity to prioritize his many inspirations. His physical responses, his cognition, and his sense of what is meaningful to him can help him. He may feel more grounded and purposeful and less fragmented as he comes to know his limitations and his potential and as he begins to connect with his inner self as well as with other people.

Profile: ENTP

Juanita exuded charm and enthusiasm. Today, in her therapist's office, she spoke quickly, articulately, and with clarity. It seemed as though her mind were racing in all directions as she spoke, and her therapist wondered how she could help her slow down.

"Last year," Juanita began, "I left my job. It was my third job in five years, so I decided that this time I needed to try working on my own. I've always wanted to do that, so for six months now, I've been working as a consultant, and I love it, but the money is a problem. An old friend loaned me some money to help me with my first year, but the money's almost gone. I've only had one break-even month, but I can't go back to my old job—even if they would take me back. If I went back, I would die. It was so boring. Every day was the same, and the people were boring, too. How can people live that way? How can they be so dull and uncreative? In that job, I lived with constant headaches, and life's too short for that—at least it's too short when you're 40. The way I'm living now, I have to live from day to day not knowing where the money is coming from, but I can do this. I'm glad I can live this way and don't have to worry about every little thing. Yet I am a little anxious, and I guess I also don't know what else I can do if this business fails. Maybe that's why I've come here."

Glad to finally have the opportunity to speak, Juanita's therapist told her that she admired her adventurous, enthusiastic spirit—even though it might also be problematic. Juanita said she understood how it could be a problem, for it was her need (and her husband's lack of need) for an interesting life that, among other things, had led to their separation.

"When was this separation?" her therapist asked.

"Last year, just before I left my job," Juanita continued. "Life was on hold. I didn't know what was wrong, but I knew I had to change it. I couldn't stand the stagnation, so I changed my job and my marriage. You know," she continued, "I think that is what causes such a lot of turmoil in our whole society—stagnation. This morning on my way to work I happened to tune in one of those radio talk shows. They were talking about the increasing rate of change in our country. I think when things get too stagnant, then we have to change. Don't you think that's true?"

Juanita's therapist asked her to talk about her marital difficulties.

"My marriage was not really a marriage," Juanita responded. "We had a lot of problems. I've tried to understand what went wrong. I'm sorry it didn't work out, and I'm also sorry my job didn't work out. I really don't want to grovel around a lot in this sentimental stuff, like a lot of my friends do. I mean, I'm sorry, but I did what I could about the situation. It's over, and I just want to make a success out of my situation now."

Juanita's therapist thought Juanita would probably be able to make a success of things, but not yet. Before she would be able to, she would need to slow down long enough to recognize old patterns and stop repeating them. She would really have to examine her situation, not just in a global objective manner but in a very personal way. She would have to accept some responsibility for her failures. She would have to find out what really mattered to her. She would have to see what was possible for her and find specific incremental steps to make things happen. This would take time and might not be something she would find exciting.

"Coming to break old patterns and establish new ones takes some time," her therapist said.

Juanita thought that was depressing. She wondered whether she wanted to deal with her misgivings and difficulties. She didn't know if she wanted to face her deep feelings, which seemed unknown and frightening to her. She wondered how was she supposed to do that.

Juanita's therapist told her that before they met again she wanted Juanita to inventory how she was spending her time. She wanted her to keep a diary of her activities, and then rate them according to their importance. She also wanted her to note times she felt bored and dull, and when she was "off track." She wanted her to pay attention to her body. If she felt physically uncomfortable, her therapist wanted her to notice what she was doing at that time. She wanted her to write all these instances down—whether she wanted to or not—and bring the list with her to their next appointment.

Her therapist wondered to herself if there would be a next appointment. She asked Juanita how she could motivate herself to be attentive to this assignment.

Summary of Observations: ENTP

- Juanita's gifts of expansiveness, assurance, enthusiasm, and her sense of adventure are both positive and negative.

- Juanita defends herself against personal confrontation with hard issues by making global, cognitive deviations.

- Juanita needs to explore in depth some of the difficulties in her marriage and career.

- Juanita needs to make a commitment to persevere.

- Juanita needs to focus on and live in the present by using her body and emotions as a guide to help her identify what is most important to her.

- Like many ENTPs, Juanita needs to focus on accountability.

Analysis: ENTP

Juanita's marital problems and continuing career difficulties require her to face difficult issues and therefore invite her to a growth adventure. If she can see it as an adventure, she may be able to accept the invitation. In her failures, which she finds difficult to examine, lie the possibility of discovering her future potential.

Juanita does not like failure and darkness, and she's afraid to look at her deep feelings and motivations. To her, it is foreign territory. She usually attacks situations and then moves on, and on one level she is able to do this with grace and charm. She knows she is moving into new territory when she moves toward inner examination rather than takes outer action. Like most intuitive thinkers who are placed in unfamiliar places, she feels incompetent in this new place. She feels movement is too slow, and she fears being overwhelmed with sentimentality, which is the way she perceives her feeling function. She sees feeling, particularly introverted feeling, as maudlin—not necessarily because it is, but because her own undeveloped introverted feeling sometimes operates that way. She is destined to repeat her unsuccessful patterns until she faces them.

In typological terms, Juanita needs to honor her auxiliary introverted thinking function and its need at midlife to set some kind of framework and boundaries around her rather energetic extraverted intuition. This can be done by naming and prioritizing the interests, ideas, and inspirations that her intuition provides.

Juanita also needs to develop her feeling function to help her realize the personal cost of not prioritizing things according to what really matters to her. It seems that her extraverted feeling is somewhat developed, allowing her to perceive to some extent what other people feel and think is important, but she finds it difficult to express her own emotions. Her introverted feeling appears unable to readily recognize her emotions: She doesn't even like to *think* about her feelings. She also has a great fear of introverted feeling, both because of its sentimental quality and because of the power it holds and the way it slows her process. Introverted feeling, with its depth and focus, seems very slow when compared to the quickness of extraverted intuition, and it is threatening to her because of the power of "heart energy."

Juanita's well-developed extraverted intuition responds quickly to things. It can generate options and offer enthusiasm for all of them. It leads to action, yet it does not lead to much discrimination. In order to achieve discrimination, Juanita needs to develop and utilize her introverted thinking. It can help her identify and evaluate consequences, but she also needs her introverted feeling to make a connection between her actions and her personal values and to acknowledge her extreme dislike of the mundane and her need for stimulation. Her introverted sensing might also aid her (as well as cause her difficulty) if she can recognize its value. Introverted sensing might help her see that life is continuity, as well as great leaps and jumps. It might lead her to see the scenes of life flowing together like the scenes of a movie, rather than as disconnected snapshots. It can be helpful for her to see that there can be adventure in a slow, thoughtful, careful life process, and it might help her honor service as well as awareness and creativity and accept stillness as well as movement. Her introverted sensing might offer her different data than her imagination has been able to offer her. It might alert her to what she can learn from her body and her life experiences.

Juanita's current midlife task requires her to break her pattern of nonreflective action and find her inner core of values on which she can focus and ground her choices. She may come closer to her center and feel enthusiastic and productive when she finds the connection between her inner self and her external actions—between flow and structure and expressiveness and focus. She will feel more competent and less fragmented when she can sort through things, focus on them, and act deliberately with personal purpose and meaning.

Typological Descriptions: ENFP and ENTP

ENFP	*ENTP*
Loving beginnings and hating endings	*Life is an audition, not a pilgrimage*
Dominant extraverted intuition	Dominant extraverted intuition
Auxiliary introverted feeling	Auxiliary introverted thinking
Tertiary extraverted thinking	Tertiary extraverted feeling
Inferior introverted sensing	Inferior introverted sensing

Their dominant intuition enables extraverted intuitives to live in a constantly changing world of infinite possibilities that fuel their enthusiasm, innovation, and energy. Their ability to make mental leaps helps them make idealogical leaps—to generate ideas and enjoy the challenge of juggling many activities at once. Focusing on and trusting the process, they prefer to remain open to all options as long as possible. They thrive on constant change and are energized by a sense of spontaneity that enables them to adapt comfortably to their environment. Neither long-range planning nor developing strategies appeal to them as much as just taking action and seeing what happens as a result. Extraverted intuitives think well on their feet, picking up external cues by hearing what is not said and seeing what is not there. After quickly sizing up a situation, they anticipate the potential obstacles and quickly take action to offset them by looking for alternatives.

When they are stressed and under pressure, their intuition may provide them with either an overwhelming number of options or very few —and often negative—ones. When their intuition leads them in too many directions, they may become increasingly scattered and thus feel compelled to escape from the disorganization and chaos as an important route to improving the quality of their life. At midlife, their range of interests may narrow slightly as they learn to focus on and sort out which options are most important and feasible to them. Their deep sense of optimism generally assures them that all situations will resolve themselves satisfactorily.

For both types, extraverted intuition—which reflects more of their outer world of change, variety, and new possibilities—is not necessarily synonymous with trusting their intuition. With increased inner focus during midlife, however, they may move toward becoming more open to the intuitive messages that come from within themselves as well as those that come from external sources. This process also puts many people in touch with their inner spiritual selves in new ways. Then they can move toward seeing the experience not as a negative crisis but as a positive challenge. Sometimes, however, their enthusiasm can mask issues that they need to confront, such as attentiveness to their physical well-being and their surroundings.

For both extraverted intuitive types, inferior sensing can have a negative quality. Overdoing and exaggerating anything, such as eating, can result from lack of contact with their inferior sensing and an overemphasis on experiencing as many external possibilities as they can, often to the point of excess. They may also become quickly overwhelmed by too much detail and angry when their inferior sensing keeps shifting all the facts. For both types, the negative side of inferior sensing may also mean "falling into the opposite." Thus, under stress, they may experience an irrational need for possessions, buying totally inappropriate clothes or gadgets that they will never use. At midlife, they may realize that buying material goods is an unsuccessful strategy for coping with stress.

Positive integration of their sensing function, however, helps them feel more authentic and grounded in who they are. By slowing down the pace of life occasionally, they are able to focus on the moment and appreciate it for what it is. Respecting limits, handling one thing at a time, setting short-range and intermediate goals, and increasing their awareness of the stress-related physical symptoms they experience are all part of integrating

sensing. By releasing tension through activities such as exercise, meditation, and enjoying the beauty of nature, they may come to feel increasingly
centered and whole.

ENFPs

Although the expected pattern of development indicates that feeling
is usually introverted for ENFPs, they often report that they extravert both
their feeling and intuitive functions during the first part of life. They
constantly expand their circle of friends, reaching out to enjoy the
company of many others. They often define themselves as being the one
who helps others, who listens, cares, and is around when others need them.
Their image of themselves often becomes an extension of their roles and
relationships as they engage in taking care of others by putting on a happy,
helping persona. Others generally value and reward their extraverted
feeling, their outwardly positive outlook, and their seemingly constant
availability to others. For some, keeping busy by being responsive to
others' needs can become a way to avoid confronting their own inner
struggles. Instead of looking for answers inside themselves, they tend to
gather information from talking to others, belonging to various groups,
attending workshops, retreats, and classes, and reading self-help books to
see what others recommend.

Their NF temperament also tends to support their extraverted feeling.
By focusing on relationships and possibilities for people, they are encouraged to find their sense of identity through their relationships with others
and affiliations with the many groups they belong to. As they receive
increased validation for their interpersonal skills, they often continue to
be pulled toward using their feeling preference to relate to others. When
stressed, however, although seeming to reach out to others, they are often
insensitive to other people's needs. They may also pay insufficient
attention to detail and to the physical world, thinking themselves into
tangled webs where all possibilities seem gloomy. When their intuition

shuts down, ENFPs may become temporarily immobilized, spiraling further into a hopeless depression. The only way they may eventually recover is by consciously seeking interaction with others. Outwardly focusing on other people's needs and keeping busy can therefore become an excuse for neglecting their inner feeling function.

At midlife, therefore, they often seek increased congruence by learning to find their own inner core and being more open to the intuitive messages that come from within them. When they put aside their outer focus temporarily, they can become focused enough to listen to, appreciate, and trust their intuition and be more open to insights from their unconscious. They seek to turn any failure into a challenge by transforming it and moving ahead. Other people enhance this process for ENFPs by telling them about their own experiences as a way of helping ENFPs make sense of their own experience. For them, the healing happens in the telling.

For ENFPs, increasing the understanding, integration, and appropriate use of their thinking function can then support their introverted feeling values. Although the strategies may seem foreign to them, the assets of thinking can help them realize that they can't be all things to all people. The objectivity of extraverted thinking may encourage them to become less responsible for all of the needs of their families and refuse to become involved in unhealthy relationships. As they become more comfortable with their thinking function, it can support their values by convincing others to affirm the things that are most important to them.

ENTPs

Internally, ENTPs may feel unassertive and are often amazed when they discover that others may see them as threatening and hard. Like other NTs, they pride themselves on being independent and seeking their own directions. For them, following instructions is akin to cheating. They enjoy being competitive and getting in the last word. Since ENTPs expect crises to be a part of life, they have less need to control them and are often stimulated and challenged by them. However, they need to construct some kind of framework that can help them make sense of their experiences. During the first part of life, they tend to analyze their emotions objectively from a thinking perspective.

Development of their feeling function may help ENTPs identify their own values, become more connected with their own emotions, and pay increased attention to personal relationships. They don't talk readily about personal things and are not likely to relate much about themselves to others. Their action orientation, to keep moving and busy as a way to avoid dealing with feelings, is often used as a way to protect the inner part of themselves. They tend to focus on projecting a positive image to others, often at the expense of denying or ignoring any emotional pain they may be experiencing. They minimize their inner reflection and allow the situation to resolve itself.

As ENTPs move toward midlife, they tend to integrate more of their thinking auxiliary, using it to support their intuition. They are enthusiastic about the intellectual challenge of understanding what's happening, seeking knowledge within a framework that will help them clarify their experience. During this period, ENTPs often experience tension between their desire to stay open to possibilities and their need to control the outcome of things. As they blend their intuition and thinking together into a partnership, however, they are increasingly able to let go and see what happens by using a minimum of control. They tend to prefer clear objectives, coupled with the freedom and autonomy to accomplish the objectives in their own style with little interference from others.

At midlife, they are increasingly drawn to integrate their feeling function, which they see as primarily an inner task. Formerly drawn more to the inner lives of others than themselves, they may be unfamiliar with their own inner life. Sorting through their personal values, they learn to know more about who they really are, but it may still not be easy for them. At midlife, they often experience an increased need for intimacy, becoming increasingly willing to share more in their relationships through self-revelation. Becoming more aware and accepting of their own personal pain and negative feelings, in midlife they often recognize a sense of freedom in knowing that they need not always be emotionally positive.

The Midlife Transition: ENFP and ENTP

Extraverted Intuitive Style: Life Is an Adventure

ENFP

Every cloud has a silver lining.

ENTP

Is it important or merely interesting?

Characteristics of ENFPs and ENTPs

- Dramatic life changes in relationships, careers, and lifestyles
- Optimism and excitement about new possibilities, even in face of difficult anxiety-filled times
- Tendency to alter outer situations rather than attend to inner situations
- Impatience with a detailed step-by-step approach to problem solving and goal setting

Particularly True for ENFPs

Need for approval from others

Particularly True for ENTPs

Need to name and understand

Relationship Issues

Other people (depending partially on their own type preferences) may

- Experience them as difficult to "ground" and resistant to long-term diligence
- Find that they are resistant to anything that seems to contain, limit, trap, or bore them

Others should try to

- Understand their own needs and biases and be empathetic to the person's resistance to limitations and boredom
- Appear enthusiastic and open to possibilities and the person's nonlinear approach to problem solving

Particularly with ENFPs, others should	*Particularly with ENTPs, others should*
Affirm them by demonstrating interest and enthusiasm for their ideas and for them as people	Respect their charm and creativity and appear intelligent and open

Guidelines for Helping ENFPs and ENTPs Through Midlife

Recognize and confirm the strengths of extraverted intuitives—their vision, breadth, energy, enthusiasm, and ability to see possibilities and connections

Particularly with ENFPs, others should try to confirm their	*Particularly with ENTPs, others should try to confirm their*
Ability to understand and affirm others	Ability to conceptualize new ways of doing things and communicate them

Encourage balance to extraverted intuitives (which will also help them develop their sensing skills) by

- Encouraging focus and limitations
- Encouraging "inner work" (i.e., looking within oneself as well as to outside sources for data)
- Requiring accountability and follow-through
- Encouraging recognition and acceptance of pain as well as joy
- Encouraging integrating one way of doing something with another rather than substituting one way for another
- Encouraging acceptance of "everydayness" and the "giveness" of things

Particularly Helpful for ENFPs	*Particularly Helpful for ENTPs*
Encourage them to gain trust of their inner self to "sort" and prioritize rather than rely exclusively on the approval of others	Encourage them to accept their own personal experience as a guide rather than rely exclusively on "cerebral" understanding

121

Profile: INFP

"I feel like I can't move," Lynn said to her friend. "It's as though I'm in the middle of a circle and all around me are choices, but I can't move toward any one of them. I feel drawn toward one and then toward another, but I also feel nailed to the center. I want to move, but I can't. None of the options work for me."

Lynn described her situation in an almost casual manner. She spoke with little energy, but strong emotions seemed just below the surface. The inconsistency and incongruence between what Lynn said and the tone she spoke with was evident.

"You're just stuck," Lynn's friend told her, trying to identify Lynn's problem much too definitively and hastily.

"Yes, but not the way you make it sound," Lynn said. "I'm not just stuck. It's like I've got to move. I can't stand it here like this. I keep hoping for some clarity, but it won't happen. The confusion just goes on and on. How long can I hold out? Is there no relief?"

"What are the urgent decisions?" her friend asked her. Bristling at the word *decision*, Lynn explained that she wasn't interested in decisions. She wanted to explore her feeling of being stuck.

"Being stuck is awful. It's like holding in a flood. It's like swimming in a kelp bed, knowing there is clear water underneath, but not being able to get to it." After a period of silence, she continued. "Why can't the world be a better place? Why do I have to struggle with it all the time? I've tried to be a good daughter, a good wife, and a good team player at work. I've tried to be me, too, but now I *must* be me. I can't do what I've been doing for years. I can't be something just because others want me to, and I'm tired of trying to get around them. I went to law school and even tried to practice. But I can't do it."

Lynn's pain and her sense of isolation and alienation were apparent. She spoke of "them"—the people she couldn't be like—and how it felt to be alienated from the world.

Some of the "them" that she felt alienated from were her friends. They wanted to talk about their houses and their children and their trips. She didn't have time for that. Lynn needed to talk about herself, but she didn't want to offend them, so she just tried to avoid them. She made up excuses for not being with them. Her husband was another person she felt alienated from. He enjoyed attending football games, and she felt he even sometimes took another person's position against her when there were disagreements. She felt that he rarely really supported her. She resented this, since she believed she had tried to be a good wife, even if she wasn't able to live up to all his expectations. And her children's school was a problem for her. She described the teachers and the administration as the most uncreative people she had ever known. She also felt alienated from her church. She felt her church had somehow "missed the boat." They talked about God and appeared to believe that "God could be explained with words." They conceptualized a God somewhere "out there." For Lynn, God was a mystery somewhere within her—at least the God she could know and relate to. Lynn didn't know whether there was a God "out there," nor did she particularly care. The spiritual was close at hand for her. Her pain, condemnation, and alienation were all there.

Lynn didn't speak for a long time, and then when she did, she spoke slowly and softly. "Some days it's an almost unbearable world to live in. Why is there such a gap between how things should be and how they are? Sometimes I don't think I can stand it anymore. I try to go my way. I try not to get too connected with people because it hurts too much, but it's also lonely to be left out. Yet I believe that there must be some lesson in all this. I always believe that regardless of how difficult things are."

She mused about what the circle might have to teach her. What was the meaning of feeling locked in the center of a circle, unable to move? What was the meaning of her sense of confusion and her lack of clarity? She wondered if she could eliminate some options and move toward others. She knew it would be hard, but she also knew the consequences of not doing so. Perhaps she could look at each possibility and explore her feelings about it and consider how much it mattered to her. Perhaps she could consider what might happen if she were to act on her options.

She knew this process would take time, but she also understood it. One day she called her friend to share her realization. "I want to connect with some of the choices around the circle, but I also don't want to connect with them. I want to be a part of my world, but I'm afraid I won't be able to be me when I do. Will I ever be able to move?"

Her friend, though not totally clear about where Lynn was heading with her observations, was confident that she would resolve her problem. She knew that when Lynn had fully considered her situation she would be able to take action.

Summary of Observations: INFP

- Lynn's matter-of-fact description of her circle image demonstrates her decision-making difficulty but misses her emotional intensity.
- Lynn rejects quickly moving toward a definition and focus because she wants to explore her feelings at the moment.
- Her accommodation/personal authenticity conflict, which has always been present, has become more demanding at midlife.
- Lynn's resistance to conformity leads her to withdraw from others and feel isolated.
- Lynn finds her repressed strong emotions frightening and explosive.
- Lynn's conflict between idealism and reality brings feelings of condemnation and pain.
- After she expresses her feelings, Lynn can begin to focus (in this case, on her values and the consequences of her actions), which she should find helpful.

Analysis: INFP

Lynn is temporarily unable to move. Basically a strong, competent person, she is now faced with decisions and feeling painfully immobilized. She experiences conflict and both fears and desires focusing on it.

She intuitively knows the cost of being aware of the conflict. One thing she fears is that she will have to "sell out" her true self in order to be connected to an imperfect external world; and, in fact, this has at times been her tendency—she has tended to try to either accommodate or to withdraw from external demands. She has not been able to comfortably be her true self in the everyday world. Her deep need for inner authenticity and her desire for connectedness with others (traits she shares with many NFs) are in a powerful struggle.

Lynn also fears that too much focused awareness will make everything less than it is. She desires clarity, but not at the expense of richness and complexity. At least complexity and openness don't make things too small. Yet complexity and openness have painfully immobilized her. Her task now is to find a way to explore her options so that she can choose without feeling that her choices are too limiting.

Lynn does not need answers or even an immediate, clear, and concrete focus. Instead she needs permission and encouragement to accept the way she feels in the moment and to search widely. Eventually, she may need help with focusing, and she will need encouragement. She needs some quiet and time to nurture her inner life so that her inner values can become real to her, offer her a basis for decision making and a voice to speak with in the external world. She also needs to let herself feel angry with a world that doesn't appreciate her, and with herself for expecting it to be so accepting. And she needs to develop a loving, safe, and accepting relationship in which she can explore, as well as a trusted relationship that can challenge her unrealistic expectations.

In typological terms, Lynn's natural introverted feeling preference will be her greatest asset—it will not only give her the data she needs; it will also help her to feel authentic and welcome. Because of her need to accommodate her outer world, her introverted feeling has not been receiving as much honor and attention as it deserves and may be ineffective from lack of use and may therefore seem a bit uncontrolled when she does use it. When her introverted feeling can be freed, it can provide her with vision, direction, and confidence, and it can place some limits on her expansive extraverted intuition by identifying what she really values. She may find her introverted feeling through journal writing, meditation, story telling, music, and art, as she tells and retells her story and feels that it is being heard.

Paradoxically, not only can her feeling function limit her expansive intuition but her intuitive function, which is multifaceted and naturally resistant to reductionistic tendencies, can also aid her introverted feeling and prevent her from holding on too strongly to her deeply held values. Her intuition, which can hold many possibilities, may help her to see that life is neither inner authenticity nor outer adaptation, but is rather an ever-fluctuating relationship between the two. It can also provide her with optimism and hope for things that often seem bleak and without hope, and may suggest creative ways to transcend the paradoxical disparity between inner and outer worlds, the self and others, and good and bad.

She has used the skills that her thinking function provides her with (e.g., to weigh the consequences of expressing her strong emotions, among other things), and they can continue to serve her in helping her to judge which of her actions are appropriate. Thinking can also provide her with some degree of objectivity to her way of being and help her realize the limitations of being excessively subjective. It might help her see things in a broader rather than a purely personal context. If she can nurture her thinking function and develop her skills, it can also enable her to confront her thoughts and feelings appropriately rather than hold them inside until they explode. Thinking can also help her see the consequences of demanding perfection in herself or others.

Her sensing can also aid her. It can give her a concrete focus and a global awareness, and it may help her express her discontent in a way that will be receptive to others. It may also lead her to take action when she discovers that she can speak of and deal with such concrete things as inappropriate career choices or career environments and inappropriate choices of friends. Sensing can translate awareness into action—admittedly in the form of incomplete awareness followed by imperfect action. Lynn's sensing might also bring her joy—and help relieve some of the intensity in her life. She may find joy in watching a sunset, drinking a cup of tea, or noticing the details in a piece of art. It may help her to live in the present and relinquish her excessive demand that things be what they are not.

Lynn's midlife task requires that she recognize and honor the personal values that her dominant introverted feeling can present. She will be nearer to her center and will feel less isolated, alienated, and misunderstood and will feel more confident, spontaneous, centered, and authentic when she is able to honor her own values and make choices based on them, even if she is in a world that may not understand them.

Profile: ISFP

Freida quietly introduced herself to a life/work planning class: "My reason for being in this class is that I want to get some control over my life." Her statement was clear, but it didn't seem complete. Other class members encouraged her to say more. "I want to learn to live alone and be happy doing that," she continued. "I'm a widow, and my children have left home. My job isn't satisfying, either. I work for a large firm that exemplifies the original old-boys' network, and I'm discriminated against because I'm a woman. There is no fun in my life. I've got to do something about it."

As she introduced herself, there was a sense of panic under her calm, quiet, gentle presence. It was difficult for her to admit that her life was in trouble, and it was obvious that Freida was not the type of person who was prone to exaggerate. The danger for Freida is not that she makes mountains out of molehills, but that she allows the molehills to develop into mountains before she acknowledges them. This was not the case for Freida right now, however. It was clear that she would need to do more than just learn how to live happily alone or stop the discrimination. Nevertheless, these represented a starting point, and they were immediate and real concerns for Freida. Could she focus on these concerns as well as look beyond them? Would she lose interest if she were drawn far away from these current concerns?

In her class, students completed a battery of self-assessment instruments that encouraged them to look at their interests and skills patterns, explore family and social messages concerning how they were expected to live and work, look at personality structure and typology preferences, explore values and life patterns and ways to cope with change, and investigate career possibilities. Freida came to class, but she said very little. One day the instructor asked each class member how the class was going for them.

"Well, I'm enjoying the group, but I don't really see how all this is helping me," Freida said. "I'm not sure what it has to do with my being discriminated against and my being lonely." She didn't see any patterns or connections.

The instructor acknowledged Freida's disappointment and expressed appreciation for her struggle with this. She told her that she appreciated the fact that Freida continued to struggle instead of leaving the class, and she said she appreciated the fact that Freida shared her feelings about the class. Then she asked Freida if she were doing the class work.

"Some of it," Freida responded. "I do it when I think it makes sense."

The instructor asked Freida what made sense to her. Freida was somewhat taken aback, but then she responded.

"I believe that if you're good and kind and try hard that you should be all right," she answered.

"You believe that if you're good and kind and try hard you won't be discriminated against and you won't be left alone," her instructor countered.

"That's the way it should be, but it isn't," Freida said.

Freida knew how she felt things should be, but she also knew and accepted that things were not as she thought they should be. She felt that kindness and gentleness should be rewarded, but she also recognized that loneliness and discrimination existed.

The class wondered what Frieda might do to alleviate her sense of loneliness and discrimination. She was asked to share with the class an example of a work situation in which she felt the old-boys' network discriminated against her and left her out. The class promised to listen to her situation and brainstorm ways that she might have handled the situation or things she might have said that would not have left her feeling so discounted. Freida was grateful that the class was willing to work concretely with her on her pressing concerns.

"I appreciate that you're trying to help me," she told the class, "but I'm going to do something about my life next week. I'm going on a golfing vacation with two friends, and when I return I'm going to look for another job, whatever job I can get that will make ends meet and let me enjoy my life."

The class was silent. They all imagined Freida a week after her vacation. It might be true that she needed a new job—one that was better suited to her. And while she certainly needed to enjoy her life more, her classmates and instructor found themselves unable to respond to her plans. They saw the "new job" as yet another unexamined choice, yet another action taken without contemplation.

"You're afraid that this won't work for me," she told them.

They nodded.

Summary of Observations: ISFP

- Freida's concise definition of her problem frames her situation, but in an incomplete manner.

- Freida needs to recognize and express her feelings before they develop into crisis proportions.

- Freida needs her class to help her meet her immediate needs and at the same time broaden her outlook.

- Freida's tendency is to accept situations without confronting them or to walk away from them.

- Freida tends to do only those things that make sense to her, but she needs to be held accountable for things she may not feel make sense also.

- Freida's idealistic and gentle nature is grounded in the world as it is.

- Examining a particular situation to take possible action (a process that often involves assertion) can help Freida, provided it does not limit her exploration of options too early.

- Freida appears unable and unwilling to continue her struggle or deal directly with her conflict.

Analysis: ISFP

Freida's considerable discomfort, which she has a hard time expressing, brings her to a counseling class. The cumulative effect of the distress she has experienced in her personal and professional life has disrupted her usual way of coping—accepting the world as it is and avoiding confronting what seems wrong. Her tendency to fit in, go with the flow, and be present in the world of ordinariness has protected her from experiencing great pain and has prevented her from doing what she says she wants to do— take control of her life. Her customary method of altering her external world whenever problems arise has given her some sense of control, but she is now at least sometimes aware that real control over her life may come from a different source. Paradoxically, her dissatisfaction with her personal life and work on the one hand and her general tendency to go along with things the way they are on the other hand have set the stage for what appears to be passivity and feels like aggression. It's as if she comes to the table but doesn't eat.

In typological terms, Freida can benefit from nurturing her dominant introverted feeling function, which can guide her toward the things that really matter to her and can give her true pleasure and fulfillment. To do this, she will need to spend a lot of time concentrating on what she needs in her life, apart from what her family, supervisor, or community want. Both Frieda and those who help her will need to refrain from taking quick action or approaching things with a "fix-it" mentality, even though she finds this appealing. Her feeling of being unappreciated and powerless, though unpleasant, may help her realize the necessity of recognizing what she needs to do so that she can again feel valued, connected, and powerful. Her SP tendencies toward action and quickness may make it difficult for her to refrain from trying to solve problems quickly while avoiding conflict, but her introverted feeling can help. If she can get her auxiliary extraverted sensing, with its need to survey the external world and implement things, and her extraverted feeling, with its need to please others, out of the driver's seat and make some space for her dominant introverted feeling, with its sense of personal authentic values, she may begin to feel as though she is getting some control over her life. She may also find in this process that she becomes personally motivated and sees the purpose behind all of her effort. With an increased awareness and the development of some assertiveness, she may come to "claim her place at the banquet table."

She may also be aided by her memory, another gift of introverted feeling, as well as her spontaneous reactions to things. It might be helpful for her to consider times when she did enjoy her life and feel appreciated and connected. Her extraverted sensing can make her aware of what the present is like, but her introverted feeling can add to this the wisdom of history.

Her sensing and feeling functions have served her well in many instances and will continue to do so. Her sensing will help her focus on what she is learning and how she can use that knowledge. Her sensing can help make the things she learns from her introspective search real, concrete, and immediate, and it can also bring her joy. Her love of golfing, spending time with friends, taking vacations, and having fun will bring her more happiness when they aren't used as an escape from conflict and pain. Physical activity, travel, and other diversions can bring her some satisfaction, as long as they are recognized as coping devices and not solutions.

And though she may need considerable help developing her intuitive function, it also has something to offer. She may broaden her outlook by further developing her own intuition and recognizing the intuitive insights of those who help her. She may realize that the discrimination and loneliness that she feels are not isolated entities but complex issues that relate to life patterns, attitudes, and specific life events. She may recognize the connection between "inner change" and "outer change" and the folly of engaging in the latter without attending to the former.

Her extraverted thinking function's skills, which are not easily available to her, may nevertheless help her place her deeply held subjective values in the outer world—and may even help her defend them, which is something she must do once she stops avoiding them. It may also help her understand the consequences of not attending to these values—feeling that hers is a life of reaction rather than agency and is a life that she doesn't control. Almost certainly as her ability to know and understand herself and her ability to confront when necessary increases, her hidden aggression will dissipate and her ability to take action will increase.

Freida's midlife task requires that she stop avoiding her inner self by taking unreflective action and "fitting in" and begin learning to pause and consult her own values for direction. She will find herself closer to her center and will feel less pressured, taken advantage of, and vulnerable. And she will feel more directed, secure, and in control of her life when she can wait for clarity and direction from her inner course of values and when she can act out of these values in her external world when necessary.

Typological Descriptions: INFP and ISFP

INFP	ISFP
Yearning for wholeness in self and relationships	*We just want to live and experience it*
Dominant introverted feeling	Dominant introverted feeling
Auxiliary extraverted intuition	Auxiliary extraverted sensing
Tertiary introverted sensing	Tertiary introverted intuition
Inferior extraverted thinking	Inferior extraverted thinking

For both INFPs and ISFPs, midlife frequently brings an increased appreciation of their dominant feeling preference. After having struggled frequently with having their inner feeling function validated by others in the external world, they now begin to move toward learning to value and own their "best" side. Like other introverts, they often tend to interact with others through their extraverted auxiliary, either intuition or sensing. Alan Brownsword, author of It Takes All Types, has concluded that the most difficult task of dominant introverted feelers at midlife is to express their emotions and values to others (especially to those who are closest to them) and identify what is most important to them and what guides their lives. Midlife often encourages them to be more selective by focusing on what they value most.

Although both types have three preferences in common (introversion, feeling, and perceiving), the difference between their auxiliary sensing and intuition, which they tend to extravert, also identifies their two different temperaments—SP and NF. This difference often leads people with these two types toward divergent life paths—INFPs toward more intellectual pursuits that generally focus on understanding human behavior and ISFPs toward more concrete ways of expressing their caring and interest in others.

INFPs

Since they frequently see many points of view, INFPs may have difficulty discerning what is most important to them. Since INFPs frequently resist conforming to standards they reject, they may experience intense feelings of isolation from many of their peers. Although they usually have deep convictions that revolve around a highly differentiated set of values, they rarely express them unless they are challenged. Their internal visions may be difficult for them to articulate, since reality rarely measures up to their visions. Although they tend to take criticism personally, they are usually hardest on themselves. Their emotional intensity may be draining to others, especially when they have difficulty communicating the depth of their convictions. In both personal and professional groups, however, they often set the ethical standards or guidelines for the group.

A common theme for INFPs is a search for personal meaning. The search for their real selves increases their awareness of and appreciation for who they are. With less need to maintain a socially acceptable persona, they can become more aware of their own values, learning both to cherish them and to recognize when compromise may be necessary in order to achieve what is most important to them. At midlife, INFPs often learn to extravert their feeling with increased comfort. As they become more open with others, they may reveal more of their inner warmth and understanding. Though they often have difficulty articulating their inner values and visions, during midlife they learn to share these with increased clarity and comfort.

Finding a balance between their individual differences and their need to be connected to others is another important midlife task for INFPs. As they increasingly recognize which situations feel natural to them, they can choose them with greater frequency.

Many INFPs focus on their extraverted intuition as a more effective—and often safer—way to interact with others in the external world. They tend to orient themselves instinctively to the data and wait for the pattern to emerge. Often aware that reality may not measure up to their ideals, they may use their intuition to help them accept this discrepancy by opening up other possibilities.

Although their intuition may help them see many points of view, it may also obscure their identification of what is most important to them. One INFP talked about her pain during adolescence, which focuses on fitting in and becoming part of the group by accommodating to the external environment. "I was often considered antisocial or uncaring," she explained, "when in fact, I cared very deeply about things." Upon reflection, however, she recognized that she rarely shared the depth of her convictions with anyone but a select few. Thus, the "masks" that INFPs wear for the external world may cover up the warmth of their introverted feeling. In addition, when doubting themselves, they often tend to discount their own emotions.

INFPs frequently resist conforming to standards that they reject and have strong, idealized concepts about the way they think things "should be." Therefore, they may experience feelings of isolation from many of their peers. Though generally easygoing and accepting, they may dig in their heels when they feel their deep, inner values are being challenged.

INFPs prefer working with groups and organizations that support their own values. They become intensely loyal and enthusiastic when involved in projects they support, often preferring to assume leadership positions. When comfortable in leadership roles, INFPs bring harmony, inspiration, consideration of others, and congruency to the task. When committed, they are gentle persuaders who tend to inspire and motivate others with their engaging warmth. As catalysts, they often help others discover more about themselves and about life. Using their intuition creatively, they work diligently to develop possibilities they can commit to and support. As frequent champions of the underdog, they often act as visionaries who quietly use their power to improve the lives of others.

Through their use of intuition, INFPs take in ideas and images that they process through their dominant feeling function. They need to see the big picture and want to remain open to all possible options. When focusing on intuition, they may work in spurts of energy that are interspersed with down times that they use for reflection. Though these times may be difficult for the "J" supervisors of INFPs to understand, these hiatus periods are necessary for INFPs to assimilate and integrate data. Since INFPs frequently see all sides as related, they may appreciate strategies that can help them eliminate some of the possibilities. Their extraverted thinking can therefore often help them focus on and sort out the most viable options.

Their third, or tertiary, preference is sensing. Paying attention to the data gathered by their senses is enjoyable for many INFPs. Learning to focus on the moment—to see a sunset, to be sensitive to body signals and changes and variations, and to experience a childlike enjoyment of the present—are ways INFPs learn to appreciate their sensing preference.

As mentioned before, many INFPs often use their inferior thinking in the outer world and are then often perceived as Ts, particulary in organizational environments. Their strong internal values are contained in their inner feeling. Displaying the genuine warmth and friendliness of extraverted feeling is more difficult for them and is often done selectively.

ISFPs

ISFPs also have difficulty sharing their inner feelings and often go to great lengths to protect them, except with those they trust. They keep their deep, internal values to themselves, quietly resisting efforts from others for disclosure, unless they are comfortable enough to do so. In relationships, they often find it easier to express their loyalties through actions rather than their words. ISFPs are very caring and sensitive with others, especially those who are most important to them. They value honest communication in close relationships and are often in tune with others. In work environments, they seek a cooperative atmosphere, where individuals are valued and well treated. If their work environment isn't characterized like this, they are likely to look elsewhere for one that is.

In midlife, like INFPs, they often become increasingly comfortable with expressing their feelings and articulating their values as a means of nurturing and enhancing their most valued relationships. Establishing an effective and comfortable persona at midlife may enable them to become increasingly assertive about things that are most important to them. In the workplace, they need to find positions that enable them to be true to their own values and work with others in nonthreatening environments. If they have chosen certain careers to please others, midlife may offer them an opportunity to choose more people-oriented careers as a means of validating their dominant feeling preference.

They may at first be perceived by others as aloof or reserved, since they are unlikely to contribute to discussions unless they have something specific to say. At times, they may be seen as antisocial, because of their need to spend time alone or with a select few. They are likely to acquiesce to others, even when they disagree with them. Increased effectiveness with their thinking preference may enable them to confront others more directly when necessary. By establishing a more effective and comfortable persona, they may then move toward becoming more assertive, taking increased responsibility for their own needs by expressing them and defending them when appropriate.

ISFPs can become very critical, both of themselves and others. At times, they may have difficulty moving past the angry judgments that may cause them to withdraw and berate themselves for their failures. When this occurs, they may break off relationships that they no longer comprehend or feel capable of understanding. Unlike INFPs, they are less likely to have well-developed, extraverted thinking functions, since their SP temperament leads them to live for the moment, removed from analytical, problem-solving, objective organizations.

They focus on the present, taking things one day at a time, enjoying life for what it is, not for what it might be. When involved in the present moment, they become spontaneous and energized by what is happening around them. Since they extravert their sensing, their dominant communication style is practical and full of facts and details. Constantly picking up data from their external world, ISFPs may need others to help them make connections between all the various pieces of information. Their SP temperament characteristics often make it difficult for them to learn from experience. Drawn to respond to the immediacy of whatever their environment offers, they often keep their pain and the difficulty they have finding solutions to themselves. Specific questions from others may help them sort out information, communicate more effectively, and move ahead toward appropriate integration of intuition and thinking.

In midlife, ISFPs need to seek both personal and professional roles that enable them to believe in and value their gifts, which include their natural joy of living, the gentle way that they care about others, and their ability to live intensely in the present with spontaneity and a sense of enthusiasm that can be contagious.

The Midlife Transition: INFP and ISFP

Introverted Feeling Style: Life Is Process

INFP

Life is about meaning—and often about struggle.

ISFP

We don't make mountains out of molehills.

Characteristics of INFPs and ISFPs

- Depth of feeling, which is sometimes unrecognized and often unexpressed
- An ability to live with process
- Resistance to defining and setting goals and strategies
- A deep sense of values that they have difficulty communicating

Particularly True for INFPs

Depth and intensity of feeling and an alienation from a world that deviates markedly from their vision of what it should be like

Particularly True for ISFPs

Acceptance of things as they are and an understanding of everyday reality

Relationship Issues

Other people (depending partially on their own type preferences) may

- Feel they are dealing with people who are fragile and easily hurt
- Find them to be lacking energy for and commitment to change, particularly if it involves conflict

Others should try to

- Understand their own needs and biases and be empathetic to the person's resistance to linear goal setting and objective decision making
- Support, affirm, and gently encourage them to remember their experiences and tell their stories and make the connection between what they are aware of and how they act

Particularly with INFPs, others should	*Particularly with ISFPs, others should*
Serve as an example of one who can gently focus and be grounded in present physical reality	Act as a guide with specific suggestions and ideas and alternatives

Guidelines for Helping INFPs and ISFPs Through Midlife

Recognize and confirm the strengths of introverted feelers—their depth, commitment, gentleness, and deep values

Particularly with INFPs, others should try to confirm their	*Particularly with ISFPs, others should try to confirm their*
Intensity and willingness to take risks to achieve self-growth and harmony with others	Gentleness and kindness and ability to focus on present reality

Encourage balance to introverted feelers (which will also help them develop their thinking skills) by

- Discouraging excessive subjectivity and encouraging them to learn by understanding general laws and principles as well as by their own experiences and feelings
- Being aware of instances when it is appropriate for them to make choices and encouraging them to do so
- Holding them accountable for incremental planning and follow-through (i.e., task orientation)

Particularly Helpful for INFPs	*Particularly Helpful for ISFPs*
Encourage them to live as their true selves in an imperfect world	Encourage them to encounter (rather than discount) important life events and situations

Profile: ENFJ

"I just can't get the balance right," Paula said as she sat down with her academic adviser. "I'm happy that I'm in graduate school now—it's wonderful. I love the stimulation and the challenge. The 15 years I stayed home with my children were nice, too, but I always felt like I was missing something. Even though I served on a lot of school and community boards, which were stimulating, I wanted to make more of a difference. I wanted to be seen as a professional. And school is wonderful. I just can't live without some way to grow, but my academic life and family are at war, and I don't want to be the resulting casualty. Last semester, I took a leave from school to try to get some order and harmony back at home, but I couldn't stand it. I felt as though my hands were tied behind my back. I would lash out at my children and husband in all kinds of inappropriate ways. So I'm glad that I'm back in school, but I also feel guilty and selfish. I want to take care of my family, but I also want to take care of myself."

Paula was an outgoing person who had an engaging manner and conversed easily. She had clearly thought her situation through and seemed to enjoy talking about it. She seemed enthusiastic, but she also seemed tired. She was in a hurry—there were things to do and people to see, and Paula wasn't a patient person.

Paula seemed to be running an important race, torn between keeping one eye on the goal and one eye on the crowd. She wanted to commit to the race, but she also wanted to watch the crowd. She wanted to achieve and accomplish things with everyone approving and cheering her on. Paula didn't want to miss anything, and she was using a lot of energy.

When she reflected on it, Paula didn't see herself running a race; rather, she saw herself running in circles. "I just go in circles," she told her adviser. "There are high and low points, but I can't get anywhere. I want my family and friends, and I want myself. I care about them and I don't have time for fighting with them. But I have to get this degree so I can take care of myself and my children, too, if it should come to that. My friend's husband died at 47. That stays in my mind, and I know I need to be able to take care of myself and my children financially and emotionally."

"Beyond that," she continued, "I need to know what my potential and my possibilities are; I know my life has a purpose. I don't think there's any answer to this problem, but it does help to talk to you about it. Each time I tell my story, I know it better. Nothing is more important than telling my story. My friends all listen to my story, and they're important to me; I couldn't live without them."

Paula's sensitivity, openness to sharing, and need for direction, achievement, and relationship is notable. She needs to look at her potential, her hopes, and dreams in a relaxed, undemanding way that enables her to acknowledge and validate the progress she has already made.

Paula knew she had accomplished a lot, but she didn't think it was enough. Whether she knew the cost of always feeling things were "not enough"—her sense of feeling driven—wasn't clear.

After some time, Paula admitted to her adviser that she wouldn't like it if her family and friends weren't there for her but that she would know more about herself if they weren't. She admitted that she didn't think she knew very much about herself.

"You know a great deal about your family and friends, but might knowing more about yourself also be good for them as well as you?" her adviser asked.

Paula wasn't sure. It was something she hadn't considered before.

Summary of Observations: ENFJ

- Paula feels conflict between her need for personal growth and achievement and her need to please and accommodate others.

- Paula's gifts are her ability to relate to others and her verbal expressiveness.

- Paula is impatient with slow processes.

- Helpers and support groups are especially important to Paula because of her need to tell her story and have it heard.

- Paula needs to live in the present with its everyday routine and limitations.

- Paula sees her need for introspection and assessment of her personal values as separate from the values held by others.

Analysis: ENFJ

Paula is torn between two of the most common of all conflicts—the conflict between self and others and between living in the present and living for the future. Even though this situation is frustrating and confusing for her, it holds great promise. Her particular situation provides her with the possibility of working out a new balance in her life and of learning about limitations and patience.

Paula is caring and giving. She wants to care for her family and keep harmony and order at home. Like most extraverted feelers, she is often tempted to define herself by the needs and desires of others. She knows more about the people around her than she knows about herself, and she is often torn between what they want from her and what she wants for herself.

Paula is intelligent, ambitious, and impatient, and she is eager to improve herself and her world. She wants to discover her purpose and live up to her potential, and her plans are quite extensive. But her conflicts temporarily immobilize her, and she hates immobilization.

In typological terms, the immobilization may be a gift if it can teach her something about her introverted functions. Immobilization will require that she give up her tendency to take quick action and her desire for clear direction, but it may encourage her to be reflective. Paula needs to make choices and prioritize before she can move ahead. Her introverted thinking, which is her least preferred function, might help her evaluate in very personal terms the cost and potential of each choice she must make and accept the painful and important reality that she can't be available for everyone or accomplish every goal she sets for herself. Her feeling function, if used in an introverted attitude, might also help her know more about what she values instead of what others value, which extraverted feelers tend to do. This kind of decision making, when made from a reflective point of view, can lead to more meaning and purpose and less of a feeling of running in circles.

Her thinking function may also, if she can develop some of its skills, help her arrange her world to reflect her priorities by assisting her with assertion. It may help her learn to say no to things that she wants to leave for others and to live as well as she can with the conflicts and the disappointment that this can sometimes generate.

Her sensing function might also help her if, when it is developed, she can learn how to accept things the way they are, and accept limitations. It might even bring her joy as she learns to accept the gifts of each moment. It may help her see the limits of what she can envision or become in life. It may help her live in the present as well as imagine the future. It may also help her live with who she is now and the way things are, as well as what she might become and how things might be.

Paula's midlife task requires that she integrate what she desires with her concern for what those around her desire and that she come to focus, prioritize, relax, and live the best that she can, taking one day at a time. She will be closer to her center and feel more comfortable, less driven, less conflicted, and less dependent on external affirmation when she knows that she can't and doesn't need to be everything to everyone. She'll be closer to her center when she comes to know she can love others even when she doesn't please them all the time, and when she knows that she can access inner as well as outer guidance, and when she comes to know she can only give to others what she first possesses, including herself.

Profile: ESFJ

Rachel cried as she sipped her coffee. This was unusual, since she was normally outgoing, optimistic, and cheerful. Her energy usually seemed limitless and her pace was quick. But today something was wrong. Today

Rachel wanted to talk about a problem she was having—a subject Rachel usually avoided.

"I've lost her," she told her rabbi. "She's gone. I knew she was unhappy and doing poorly in school, but I didn't expect this. She flunked out and left school. She called and said she wouldn't be coming home, that she just wanted to be away from all of us. She didn't even give me a telephone number or an address where I could reach her. I've really lost her." Rachel began to regain her usual sense of control.

She was referring to her daughter, who had run away from home. She talked—for many hours on that day and on other days—of her daughter's academic and personal problems. She blamed her daughter's school, she blamed her daughter's irresponsibility, but most of all, she blamed herself.

"I'm a failure," she continued. "I've failed as a parent, and that was the most important thing I ever had to do. I can't tell you how terrible I feel. If I knew where she might be, I would go and try to find her. I've failed."

Her rabbi wondered aloud what she meant by "failure." "I've told you," Rachel responded. "I feel like a failure, and talking a lot about it doesn't help. I need to get her back, but I don't know what to do. I feel guilty about all this, and other people seem to think it's my fault, too. My mother thinks I should have known what was happening with her before things got to this point. My husband thinks I overreact and that I'm a worrier. I am a worrier, but I don't think she'll come back. My husband actually thinks she'll come home after she thinks it over. Neither my mother nor my husband understand, and they don't know what to do. None of us has any idea where to start looking for her."

Rachel's rabbi felt as though she was asking him for solutions, and he wanted to avoid that. He told her that he didn't know where to look for her daughter either, but he wasn't ready to admit blanket failure so easily. He asked Rachel to at least entertain the idea that she might in fact not be a failure just because one of her children had experienced some difficulty, although he understood that she felt she was. He asked her about her other children and about her community work, which he found significant and impressive. Rachel didn't see what this had to do with her current problem.

With some trepidation, he asked Rachel if she were perhaps angry with her daughter for betraying her after she had devoted a good part of her life to caring for her. Rachel didn't think so. Nevertheless, he suggested that she read a book on anger, hoping that she might make a connection between self-sacrifice and the resentment she might be feeling. Together she and her rabbi established a plan that would allow them to discover what really mattered to her, along with her concern about her daughter.

Rachel wasn't sure this would help because she wanted to actually do something to help find her daughter, but she nonetheless agreed to try the strategy. Over the next several weeks, she read several books on anger and diligently tried to learn all she could about her life. She found the process interesting, though she periodically wondered what it had to do with finding her daughter.

And then in the midst of this period, Rachel had a dream. In the dream, Rachel was trying unsuccessfully to give birth to a baby. Her rabbi suggested that babies in dreams sometimes represent new life. She hadn't thought of that. She thought the dream was telling her that she couldn't be a good parent, but she liked this possible interpretation.

After some time, Rachel's daughter did return home. Rachel was greatly relieved, and she was also pleased that she had begun to form a clear idea of what her own "new life" might mean. She decided that she would finish her college degree, something she had given up when she had married and had children. It was something she never completed but would like to finish now. She realized that she had resented the fact that she had never been able to finish school. She was also surprised to learn that she wanted to be more than a wife. She enjoyed her marriage and wanted to spend more time with her husband, but she also wanted time for herself. "I want to have fun, too," she said. She thought about traveling, decorating her house, entertaining, taking aerobics classes, and going out with her husband.

Her rabbi encouraged her to pursue her action plan but suggested that she might want to evaluate her options and determine which of them she wanted to focus on, rather than attempt to take on all of them at once.

He knew that action was a strong point for Rachel and knew that it and contemplation needed to be honored. She was moving a little fast for him, but it was her pace and not his that mattered. He told her that he admired her drive and her planfulness, and that he hoped her relationship with her daughter would also continue to improve.

Summary of Observations: ESFJ

- For Rachel, as is the case for many ESFJs, difficulties in relationships, particularly parent-child ones, often initiate change.

- Rachel's natural tendency is toward blame—external and, in particular, internal blame.

- Rachel demonstrates her tendency to overgeneralize, which she often does in a negative direction.

- Rachel is often intimidated by the opinions of others.

- Rachel, in her search for a focused plan of action, fails to see the value of exploration and reflection.

- Rachel appears unwilling to face unpleasant emotions, especially anger and betrayal.

- Rachel illustrates the ESFJ gifts of follow-through and an openness to suggestions.

- Rachel needs to expand her ways of seeing things.

Analysis: ESFJ

Rachel's persona of being a good parent is abruptly taken away from her when her daughter "betrays" her. Rachel has long seen herself as a loving, devoted, hardworking parent who tries to do all the right things for her family and friends, and she has expected good results. But good results do not seem evident now. And yet while this is painful, it may offer her the opportunity to move beyond her well-developed parental orientation to find a deeper, more personal meaning for the second half of her life.

Rachel knows she is a good person because she believes she is a loving person, and people tell her she is, so it must be so. She has raised her daughter carefully, and she expects good results in return. Her daughter's actions call all these assumptions into question. Rachel feels abandoned, taken advantage of, and, in particular, guilty. She feels exposed and raw, but she does not want to examine her feelings. Instead, she is obsessed by a desire to know how to correct the situation she finds herself in. She has always been good at patching up relationships and restoring harmony, but this time she feels there is nothing she can do. Feeling immobilized and pained, she looks for someone to blame and, for the most part, blames herself. She feels that she must have done something terribly wrong for things to have turned out this way.

In typological terms, Rachel needs to utilize some of her less-developed as well as her well-developed preferences. She needs her thinking function's skills, undeveloped as they may be, to offer her some objectivity and help her to discriminate between and evaluate her options.

In particular, she needs some introverted thinking skills, with their emphasis on precision and the particular. Rachel tends to make broad assumptions and generalizations. She needs to verify her assumptions and define them more precisely. If she can develop her thinking function somewhat, she might see the folly of assuming general life failure as a result of one incident in life. Her more developed thinking function might also help her to see the extent of her participation in and her responsibility for her daughter's actions. It might help her realize that although her daughter's actions have caused her a great deal of pain, she is not defined by her daughter or anyone else.

Rachel is in tune with her dominant extraverted feeling, which is not surprising in a society that highly values extraverted feeling. It is her introverted feeling, however, if she can use it, that might help her discover what is important to herself as well as other people. Her introverted feeling might help her move toward inner as well as outer harmony. Her introversion might also slow her pace—at least to some extent—and by turning inward and slowing down she might discover some emotions (among other things) that she had not recognized because she had judged them negatively. And she may learn something about the paradoxical nature of things. She might discover both the positive and negative sides of anger. She might recognize its relational quality and its energy as well as its destructive nature. She might also see both the positive and negative side of always trying to please other people. She might see the negative side of this, with its tendency toward martyrdom, self-denial, and manipulation, as well as its relational nature.

Her intuition might also help her if she can develop it. Rachel has always wanted focus, control, clarity, and plans of action. Intuition might cloud clarity and focus and delay her plans, but it might also help her consider multiple plans and a broader view of things. It might help her see that things can work out in ways that may not be obvious to her, and that a bad mother/good mother definition is too rigid and much too limiting as a definition of self.

Rachel's midlife task requires her to recognize the danger of selling her soul for the approval or benefit of others and the need for her to expand her rather narrow views. Rachel may be closer to her center and feel less burdened when she finds that things can sometimes work out without a great deal of effort and that there may be several equally good paths to take in a situation. And she will feel free when she realizes that she can confront conflict and survive (even though she may not like it) and that even when other people may not like her or do what she wants them to, she can still like and value herself.

Typological Descriptions: ENFJ and ESFJ

ENFJ	ESFJ
Let's do it with enthusiasm and energy	*Happiness is caring and sharing*
Dominant extraverted feeling	Dominant extraverted feeling
Auxiliary introverted intuition	Auxiliary introverted sensing
Tertiary extraverted sensing	Tertiary extraverted intuition
Inferior introverted thinking	Inferior introverted thinking

Extraverted feelers orient themselves around relationships, seeking affirmation, and gaining energy from their many friends and the groups they belong to. With their great need for interaction and validation from others, they may focus on others' needs at the expense of not meeting their own. They attend to others, make them comfortable, and demonstrate their care for them through gracious warmth and hospitality. Sensitive to nuances in interpersonal relationships, they strive to make others feel good and keep the social environment agreeable to everyone. They thrive on being needed. The image of "helper" tends to dominate their persona during accommodation, since they define who they are in terms of their relationships to others. When employed, they may view their salary as the icing on the cake.

When their need for harmony leads them to sacrifice their own needs for others, they may become resentful. However, extraverted feelers are quickly reassured of the value of their roles when they receive praise, affirmation, and validation from others.

With all the advantages of their extraverted feeling, they do recognize some disadvantages to their preferences, which they often try to alleviate at midlife. They see themselves as taking strong positions on others fairly quickly—often when they have little appropriate data. Frustrated and stressed by open-endedness and deadlines, they may push for closure without seeking all the available information. At midlife, they often consciously try to alleviate their need for control by working more collaboratively.

By focusing primarily on their extraverted feeling, they often have difficulty getting in touch with their own values and emotions, which have often been repressed within them. Because they are often busy taking care of others, they may lack insight into themselves. One midlife task for many extraverted feeling types therefore is to find congruence between their own inner values and their desire to help others first.

Integration of introverted feeling presents the challenge of finding out what they really want. As they pay more attention to their own needs, they begin to restructure themselves within their relationships. Having previously sought answers primarily from the outer world, they increasingly turn within for answers, using their own values as a reference point for decision making. Resetting priorities, redefining reality, and restructuring themselves within their relationships often become important midlife tasks.

ENFJs

The search for meaning for ENFJs is a long one, but it gradually becomes less deliberate. Affirming that they are valuable in their own right, their feeling gives them new answers even without them having to formulate the questions. As with most NFs, the questions of intimacy and identity become increasingly important during this transition. They may ask themselves questions such as, "Can I remain in the context of this relationship without feeling guilty?" or, "Who am I apart from these roles?" Finding answers to issues and potential conflicts in identity and relationships can enable them to seek new visions that can replace old realities.

Asking ultimate and spiritual questions about their purpose in life helps them to refocus on their roles and trust their inner awareness. When stressed, they are often able to focus on their introverted intuition, asking themselves such questions as, "What's stopping me?", "Why can't I make this change?", and "What are the alternatives?"

Development of their sensing function may include learning to enjoy one day at a time. Slowing the pace of life helps ENFJs focus more on the moment, replacing "what if" with "what is" as they become more in touch with their senses. An increased awareness of physical stress may help them become more intentional about allowing themselves time for physical activities as a means of alleviating stress.

Their inferior thinking function can be used more intentionally to support their own personal values, helping them present their conclusions in well-thought-out ways. The valuing process of introverted feeling can help them prioritize their values. Their objective thinking may help them focus more on what is really important to them by helping them realize that they can't be everything to everyone. Thinking may also help them cope with conflict more effectively by limiting their directions, increasing their focus, and enabling them to become more objective. Often hurt by criticism, they recognize their need for positive feedback but understand the necessity of becoming less sensitive to personal criticism. By learning to live with less external affirmation, they also feel less of a need to prove themselves. Their thinking function can also help them cope more effectively and openly with conflict as they become more objective and learn to assess the pros and cons of their actions and assess the effect their actions will have on others.

ESFJs

ESFJs like everything to be planned, predictable, and orderly. Midlife, with its changing focus from "I should" to "I want," helps them feel less of a need to control events. Increased awareness of their introverted sensing may help them enjoy each moment just as it is. They tend to accept the present situation as it is and use the facts to move on and make a decision.

They are not likely to talk at length about their pain, preferring instead to take action to improve the situation, complete work on it, and then move on. Completion and closure provide them with a focus.

Their SJ temperament encourages them to structure the external environment in terms of "shoulds" and "oughts." However, they may become disillusioned when events don't go as planned. Many ESFJs have an almost obsessive need to "fix" relationships, holding them together at any cost. As supreme caretakers, ESFJs tend to reach out in response to others, often at their own expense. At midlife, they increasingly begin to take more time and space for themselves. With a decreasing need to prove themselves to others, they no longer have to make excuses for taking time for their own personal needs.

Their auxiliary sensing helps them look at the present situation as it is. Feeling increasingly grounded and accepting of who they are, they can then move on to incorporate other aspects of themselves. Finding more personal time and space for themselves decreases their need to keep busy and frees up time for reflection and becoming more centered in the present.

Integration of some elements of intuition increases their flexibility by offering them new possibilities and options. Seeking out others' ideas and perspectives may help them to recognize options. Having used their sensing function to gather facts, they can then move toward identifying new and different options, asking themselves "what if" questions. Thinking helps them evaluate options objectively by identifying the consequences of following each of them. With their dominant feeling, they can then ask themselves: "What is most important to me at this point in my life? What do I really want? What am I willing to give up in order to get it?"

Unlike ENFJs, who may find the world of concepts and ideas intellectually challenging, ESFJs tend to find the theoretical world fatiguing. Some find that crafts such as needlework or woodwork provide them with a way to feel focused and grounded. For many of them, integration of the thinking function seems to focus more on accommodating to "Ts" instead of working to integrate elements of their own thinking function. Working with thinkers on projects and trying to understand their perspective through increased communication and interaction may prove to be useful tools. Becoming more assertive about their personal values may also help them work toward further integration of the thinking function, which can help them find more effective ways to promote their personal values in their groups and organizations.

The Midlife Transition: ENFJ and ESFJ

Extraverted Feeling Style: Moving On...
With a Little Help From Our Friends

ENFJ	ESFJ
Self and others: How to be true to me and keep harmony with them.	Structure is strategy: Structure is a support system and structure is time.

Characteristics of ENFJs and ESFJs

- Feelings of guilt about spending time and energy on themselves
- Unexpressed rebellion and anger
- A search for answers in external sources, often in other people
- A quick pace

Particularly True for ENFJs	Particularly True for ESFJs
Have an enthusiasm for growth and a fear of losing relationships as a result of change	Have a deliberate, planful search for direction and a fear of losing this direction

Relationship Issues

Other people (depending partially on their own type preferences) may

- Perceive them as more in touch with how others feel than how they themselves feel
- Perceive them as impatient and quick to make judgments

Others should try to

- Understand their own needs and biases and be empathetic to the person's resistance to anything that disrupts harmony and causes conflict
- Appear to be supportive, caring, and interactive

Particularly with ENFJs, others should

Encourage them to talk about and
reflect on their personal life story
and promote in them realistic,
achievable goal setting

Particularly with ESFJs, others should

Provide them with concrete
suggestions and options, as well as
encouragement for letting go of
outgrown attachments and
risking new goals

Guidelines for Helping ENFJs and ESFJs Through Midlife

Recognize and confirm the strengths of extraverted feelers—their relatedness,
diligence, action orientation, and discipline

*Particularly with ENFJs,
others should try to*

Recognize their enthusiasm for
growth and personal resourcefulness

*Particularly with ESFJs,
others should try to*

Recognize their careful, steady
nature and their willingness to act
on new learning

Encourage balance to extraverted feelers (which will also help them develop their
thinking skills) by

- Encouraging them to nurture their own inner lives and evaluate their personal
  values apart from collective values
- Helping them live out their own truths in the face of disharmony and
  disapproval
- Encouraging them to slow down their level of activity (particularly
  caretaking) and to entertain ideas that aren't immediately pleasing to them

Particularly Helpful for ENFJs

Encourage them to feel an
appropriate acceptance of present
reality

Particularly Helpful for ESFJs

Encourage them to expand their
options and feel an enthusiasm for
new possibilities

Profile: INTP

When Antonio entered the office of the external employee assistance adviser, a sense of intensity surrounded him. His movements were controlled, but it was easy to sense that many things about Antonio weren't immediately obvious.

"My boss and I aren't getting along," he said immediately. "I've worked for him for years and we've never really gotten along, but in the last several years he has become unbearable. He is an arrogant, incompetent bureaucrat." Antonio was becoming heated. "I've reached my end with him. He can't be trusted. He'll do anything for political reasons—he talks out of both sides of his mouth and agrees with whomever happens to be present. I used to put up with some of this, even though I never liked it, but now I've really had it. Maybe I could bear him if he just once had a decent, original thought, but I've given up on that."

Antonio, who used words sparingly, was finished. The anger in his deliberately chosen words was clear. As he sat quietly, the sadness in his taut, intense expression became evident. His words had been formulated long before Antonio spoke them, and he feared that if he didn't control them his feelings might incinerate anyone in his path, or he might be reduced to tears, which would be embarrassing for him.

His adviser thought that Antonio was angry and hurt, but Antonio did not think that. He saw himself as reasonable. He saw himself moving through life with a casual kind of determination, and he was partially correct. He did not speak without thinking, and when he spoke, people generally listened. They were sometimes offended, but they generally respected what he had to say. People saw Antonio as someone who was difficult to approach. They wished he would tell them what he was thinking in a way they could understand.

When Antonio was younger, a teacher had spoken to him of his fine imagination and clear thinking. He had liked science and literature— science for its clarity and literature because he found it interesting. Interesting was an important word to Antonio, but now his work wasn't interesting. He felt it was too mundane and restrictive, and he blamed his boss for "adjusting" to it. At a deeper level, it seemed possible that Antonio also blamed himself for betraying his own gifts.

"And my work is boring," he said. "It's the same old thing—people don't get rewarded unless they butter up the powers that be. They just want a yes man, and one who says yes quickly, too. My annual review said that I don't communicate well and that I'm not a team player. It said that I'm too hard on people, especially people I don't perceive as bright. Well, most of them aren't bright, so what I am supposed to say? They won't do anything on their own and they have to be told the simplest things over and over again."

Antonio's anger was building again. "I do have trouble getting along with some of the people at work," he continued, "but I do get along with a lot of people, including my family and friends most of the time. I don't have a horde of friends, but I have enough. They let me be, and I let them be. Why can't they do that at work? My annual review said that I have excellent ideas and often offer innovative suggestions. If that's true, then why don't they accept that? Why do they want to make me into something I'm not? I can't understand that, but I'll tell you," he continued, "no one is going to make me into something I'm not."

Antonio's adviser asked Antonio what was really bothering him, believing that Antonio might be able to name it more precisely. It took some time for him to formulate his response, but Antonio knew. It wasn't long before Antonio identified what was bothering him.

"The issue is how to live with other people in a screwed up world and still be me," he responded. He paused and reformulated his response. "It's how to love and keep my integrity."

Summary of Observations: INTP

- Antonio often experiences interpersonal conflicts involving competency and integrity issues.
- Antonio fears his deep feeling responses.

- Antonio has difficulty communicating in an easily understood manner.

- Antonio has gifts of imagination, originality, and clear thinking, which he feels he is unable to use.

- Antonio finds boredom in his work unacceptable.

- For Antonio, a sense of independence—a sense of inner and outer authenticity—is essential.

Analysis: INTP

Antonio's conflict with his supervisor, someone who is very different from him and whom he can neither understand nor accept, offers him the opportunity to explore new ways of being. He does not, of course, see this as an opportunity. In his current situation, Antonio desperately wants to be himself, and he fears he cannot do this in his workplace, yet he does not appear ready to leave his job (and supervisor), which he feels are threatening his ability to be himself. With this tension there is some promise, though it feels like anything but that to him. Conflict is not a new experience for Antonio. He has often felt himself at odds with the world. At times he has reacted by withdrawing or keeping his deeply held convictions to himself. Often he fights with others about his strongly held views, sometimes without much regard for their opinions. But now for the first time at midlife he is questioning if he can both live authentically and come to value others who are different from him. He feels agitated by the question.

The agitation is exaggerated, since Antonio is traveling in new territory. His approach to life, which has worked reasonably well up until this time, has been to examine every option carefully and then arrive at definite, well-supported conclusions. He needs to understand things, which he usually does. He doesn't accept things he doesn't understand. One thing he can't understand is people he regards as unimaginative, inconsistent, or unauthentic. He can't understand how people can be so boring and too lazy to think things through or be too weak to stand up for their convictions.

In typological terms, Antonio can benefit from developing his sensing and feeling functions and by learning to extravert his introverted thinking. If he can extravert and communicate to others his careful and precise thinking process, they can better appreciate his careful reasoning and might even help him further refine it. For example, if he can discuss with his supervisor the things he experiences when his supervisor behaves inconsistently (such as a lack of trust and confusion), it might help him. He may witness some change in his supervisor's behavior or he may learn some of the reasons for the "political" behavior that he finds so disturbing. Antonio is able to understand reasons. And even if he receives no external satisfaction, he will still be moving toward communicating who he is to the world and may feel less rage and more authenticity within himself, especially if he abandons the idea that others must meet his expectations.

Antonio's intuition seems well developed, as is evident in his annual review, which commends him for his "excellent ideas and innovative suggestions." It might be hypothesized that his intuition is developed, since it is the function he meets the world with. He has used it extensively and it has served him well. And it will continue to serve him well, even as some development of his sensing function can also help him move ahead.

His sensing can ground him in the everyday world of ordinariness. If he can develop it, he may come to see things as they are as well as how they might be. He may come to live with adaptive demands as well as authenticity demands without abandoning either, and he may come to recognize the requirements of the present as well as the promises of the future. He may even come to appreciate service (and those who serve) as well as original, idea people. And because of this appreciative attitude, communication with them may become easier.

His extraverted feeling function, with its keen sensitivity to what is important to other people, might help him if he can access it to realize that other people see things through different lenses. And he might come to see that although these lenses do not have his sharp precision, they are nevertheless valid.

Antonio's major midlife task requires that he find a way to live authentically in the world without alienating it. He may feel less alienated and more connected when he realizes that he cannot clearly understand others, nor can they clearly understand him. Relaxing his judgment of others and himself may make him feel more accepted and may allow him to take the risk of communicating more honestly who he really is.

Profile: ISTP

The voice at the other end of the counselor's telephone line was agitated. "I've got to see you right away," he said. "Things are terrible at work and at home. I've got to see you now. That's why I called you at home." The counselor had an open appointment the next day.

When Bill—an attractive, athletic-looking man of 40 or so—walked into the counseling office, his counselor was surprised at his calm, almost casual demeanor. After their telephone conversation he had expected anything but an easygoing manner; nevertheless, Bill was at ease. It occurred to his counselor that people would find Bill easy to be around.

"I'm sorry I called you at home," Bill began. "But I was really upset. I felt ill at work, and my boss gave me the day off. When I got home my wife was there and she wanted to talk about my work and our relationship. I felt crazy. I'm better now, but when I called I didn't know if I would make it through the day. I have this new job," he continued, "and it's driving me crazy. I'm managing some computer technicians. Now I know how to repair computers. I used to like my work, but recently I've just been stressed out about it. I don't understand why everything's changed. I usually can understand things, but I'm losing confidence in myself. I can't understand why I'm upset all the time."

The counselor asked for more information about the difficulties Bill was experiencing at work.

"There is too much work," Bill answered. "I really don't mind work, but I'm not a workaholic. Work should be fun, but it isn't—and work is all I do now. The way I see it, work is a means to an end—it is what you do on the way to life, but now there is no life, just work. I want to be happy. I hate not knowing what people who work for me are doing. There are so many of them now, and I don't understand what they do. I spend my time in meetings and I have endless reports and projections to do. Long-range planning isn't my thing. I don't like meetings either, but I also don't like to work alone for long periods. It's boring to work alone. When people interrupt me, I'm glad—especially if they want me to help them out with a repair problem. Computers are sometimes more interesting than people," he said.

Bill felt best at work when people asked him to help them out with something he knew how to do. His new responsibilities were forcing him into areas he didn't enjoy and in which he didn't feel competent. He felt best when people asked him to fix something they were stuck with. He just did it for them. But he didn't understand people who couldn't see what was in front of them.

Remembering that he mentioned his wife, his counselor asked Bill about her. He seemed a bit annoyed with this diversion, but he responded.

"You're probing, aren't you, but I guess that's your job. She's all right. She keeps giving me books to read about careers, but I usually don't read them. They don't help, so I usually change the subject. I know she doesn't like me to do that, but what else can I do? She's a good wife, and my boss is a good guy, too. For example, I told him that I didn't like having so many new people to manage and he reassigned some of them. He even gave me part of my old job back. I like honest people who get to the point, and he is one."

Bill's counselor asked how he could be of assistance. Bill was convinced he wanted to find a different job. When asked what he had thought of as career possibilities, he responded immediately: "Pilot."

"But I've checked it out and besides all the training, I wouldn't earn as much as I do now for at least three to four years," he continued. "Dentist, maybe, but it's the same kind of situation. I don't want to go to school, and

I don't want to give up my income. I want money to do what I like. And I would like to be a builder," he went on, "but the economy isn't good, and it would take a long time to get established. That's the problem. Everything takes too long, but these jobs are what I'm interested in. I want to live now. I want to be happy now."

His counselor wondered how thoroughly Bill had researched his choices. Bill knew both a builder and a dentist, so his homework assignment was to visit them for informational interviews. He and his counselor also set up an assessment program, including some testing, to see if they could generate options for Bill. He agreed to this, although he "wanted it to be over with" and didn't care much about such things as interests, skills, and values. He didn't understand that generating options might help him reach a resolution.

His counselor asked him to think about and make a list of the things that would be necessary to make his current work acceptable to him and bring fun back into his life. He was also to make a list of the things he would need to do to bring about any of the changes he was investigating through his informational interviews. The counselor hoped that by the end of the process Bill would realize the limitations he would have to live with regarding his freedom and ability to move quickly.

Summary of Observations: ISTP

- Bill, like many ISTPs, seeks help in a time of crisis, often during a short-term crisis.

- Bill sees competently performed work as play or a means to enhance life's opportunities, rather than as having intrinsic worth.

- For Bill, competence is important and is demonstrated by direct, hands-on work, while a lack of competency (and understanding) produce anxiety for him.

- Bill demonstrates his dislike and distrust of self-examination.

- Bill demonstrates typical gifts of directness, focus, and action orientation as well as an impatience and unwillingness to delay gratification.

- Bill appears to have a tendency to forget to express his gratitude to others.

- Bill's thinking function can help him understand the cost and potential of decision making, but his SP temperament may cause him to resist a systematic decision-making process.

Analysis: ISTP

Bill's work situation draws his attention when it reaches crisis proportions. He becomes physically ill and takes a day off but finds that his wife is discontented. He deeply resents that his work has changed and that both its quantity and functions are disturbing his once-pleasant life. He is unhappy because he can't understand his feelings of discomfort and is unable to stop them. He wants to escape from his work, but he also wants to maintain its benefits.

To his credit, he is able to focus on his point of discomfort and seek help. His new job responsibilities don't seem well suited to him, and he knows he needs to make some changes. He wants to make changes, but he also wants a quick, painless solution. His immediate response is to think about a job change, but he doesn't want to spend his time contemplating new options or training for new directions, and he certainly doesn't want to lower his income or his standard of living.

Bill is both fortunate and unfortunate. He is unfortunate because his work world values and pays him to do things he doesn't want to do, such as long-range planning and other management functions. His supervisor intended to reward him with a promotion, but Bill's changing responsibilities have made him feel discontented and have forced him to make choices about income versus job satisfaction. He is also fortunate because he has an understanding supervisor and a supportive wife. He needs their help in learning about relationships as well as his unwillingness to accept stress, ambiguity, and the pain of slow process.

In typological terms, Bill's extraverted feeling function, if he can be receptive to it and nurture it, can help him understand the needs of his employer, his wife, and others. It can help him see their need for open communication, even if it doesn't appear to be immediately productive to him. It can help him see that they value "working out difficulties" rather than avoiding them and may even, because of its relational quality, enable him to contribute to the process. His feeling function, which he may find embarrassing and uncomfortable, may even help him come to appreciate and express appreciation for the efforts they make on his behalf. His introverted feeling, which may be difficult for him to access, may also help him, perhaps as much as his dominant introverted thinking, to prioritize what he values—that is, whether doing work he likes is more important to him than income and status.

Bill's personality structure does not suggest great satisfaction in traditional management positions. He is unlikely to become an appreciator of meetings or of long-range planning. His SP temperament and his typology both deny this, but if he can develop some of his NF temperament, with its tendency to be expansive and accepting, he may realize that people operate differently. An accepting attitude might help him to better understand and appreciate the need for management people and for people who are interested in focusing on relationships, as his wife is.

His intuition, if he can develop it, may help him discover many options for improving his work and his life and may help him to see that things are rarely black or white—that they are rarely either totally acceptable or totally hopeless. He may find, with the help of his intuition, that there are many facets and people to be considered when work and life are restructured.

And he will find a way to do these things with the help of a guide, because he realizes that he must. His rather well-developed sensing and thinking functions, which have been rewarded with the job promotion that has initiated his current situation, have helped him understand cost and promise. They help him understand how the world operates and though he wishes to avoid them at this moment, they help him understand limits and the consequences of choice.

Bill's major midlife task requires him to focus on his immediate concern (pain) about his work and begin the process of learning what it has to offer rather than trying to ignore it or run away from it. He will feel more at home and content when he realizes that things are not all black and white, that there are many ways of restructuring life, that we are all connected and interdependent, and that there are limits to our freedom and ability to take action. He will be closer to his center when he discovers that pain and joy are a part of most of life and that they coexist.

Typological Descriptions: INTP and ISTP

INTP	ISTP
We need incubation time, so new life can appear	*Play with me, but don't try to control me*
Dominant introverted thinking	Dominant introverted thinking
Auxiliary extraverted intuition	Auxiliary extraverted sensing
Tertiary introverted sensing	Tertiary introverted intuition
Inferior extraverted feeling	Inferior extraverted feeling

Both INTPs and ISTPs use their dominant function best in the introverted world, but how it plays out seems to rely heavily on their auxiliary functions. Both types focus on material that is logical, rational, and objective. Both types recognize their need for sufficient introverted time to sort out information and formulate a judgment based on logic; both also often report having difficulty identifying their feelings. Increased integration of their inferior feeling can enable both types to become aware of their personal interactions and their impact on others, as well as identify what is most important to them.

For both types, development of their inferior feeling function becomes increasingly important. They tend to be very loyal to those who are special and important to them and show their feelings in little, subtle ways. With those who are not close to them, they often seem detached, appearing uncaring and reticent, especially with people they don't know well. Often hard on themselves, they also tend to be critical of others. They tend to be very tolerant of others until a specific issue touches something they care deeply about. In such cases they can preserve their values and be uncompromising. Both types can experience difficulty with interpersonal skills. In midlife, they recognize the need to say what they mean and listen to the feedback of others, as well as the need to alter their positions in response to the needs of others. Introverted thinkers talk about their difficulties with relationships. Often ignoring their own emotional needs, they often also don't enable others to know much about them. At midlife, they should try to maintain their inner sense of integrity while becoming more accepting of others. Through this process, they can then become less judgmental and increasingly available to people they have relationships with.

INTPs

INTPs thrive on developing theories and frameworks. They use models as tools to organize their information, focusing on designing organizational systems and grand schemes, which may need further interpretation by others in order to make them accessible. Prior to communicating their ideas to others, they first need to achieve inner, intellectual clarity for themselves. Like some other thinking types, INTPs may learn to identify their emotions by paying attention to sensing, physical clues.

INTPs, like ISTPs, talk about their need for sufficient introverted time before reaching closure. At other times, if they have already thought through their ideas, they may make a lightning-fast analysis, although they often keep it to themselves at first. When they stall for time, they take whatever time is necessary to organize information objectively. Often this pattern can cause misunderstanding when it results in a withholding of ideas until they are prepared to share them. Some INTPs report that when they do speak they tend to do so quickly out of fear that they will be cut off before they have sufficient time to express their thoughts. Once they feel they have carefully thought out their ideas, they may respond defensively when their logic or ideas are challenged. At mid-life, they often become increasingly aware of their need for extraversion earlier in the process as a way to stay in touch with reality by getting feedback.

Consistent with Jung's theory of individuation, many INTPs have talked about their tendency to accommodate to the requirements of others during the first part of life. Although some feel the need to get along with others in the external world, they often resent it and internalize their anger. They often reduce stress by learning to value and accept their extraverted auxiliary intuition, relying on their dominant introverted thinking primarily in times of crisis or when they have sufficient introverted time to process ideas before anticipating them. By spending more time focusing inward at midlife, they may come to value their dominant function and use it with greater confidence in the outer world.

Another important issue for INTPs is the need they have to maintain their inner integrity, preserve their own values, and be true to themselves. In their personal relationships, they seek to find a balance between critiquing and loving. Often critical of both themselves and others, they have high personal standards and expect those close to them to meet them. Their development at midlife centers around independence, respecting their own needs, and refusing to sell out to goals imposed by others. Worldly success is of little value for its own sake, unless it is accompanied by independence and a respect for their inner sense of who they are within an atmosphere that allows them maximum flexibility.

For them, the midlife transition is not something new. As one INTP put it, "we've been in transition most of our lives. We've been seeking all along, almost waiting for the world to catch up with us and accept us." Some INTPs never reach this point, and they don't stay in jobs or relationships long enough to reach the point when they can be appreciated.

ISTPs

In contrast to INTPs, ISTPs often talk about taking on the role of observer as a way to collect appropriate data. They tend to trust only concrete data from their senses, focusing on the practical application of that data. They know how to ask the right questions in order to get whatever pertinent information they need. Often becoming irritated by conversations embellished with minor, unnecessary details, they prefer to get to the point of the issue as soon as possible. As observers, they need sufficient introverted time for sorting out their information in order to formulate a logical judgment. They tend not to disclose their insights unless they are questioned, are in a crisis situation, or are responding to something that is important to them. They may first need to be convinced of the need for change and are often unwilling to institute change unless it appears necessary.

Sensors tend to be impatient with theory, seeking a logical framework for dividing information into categories and sorting details and facts. They need to understand how things work and have little interest in theoretical concepts for their own sake. Often impatient with theory, they need to see its practical value. They may ask themselves questions such as "What can I do with it?", "How does it apply?", and "How can it help me solve this problem?" They have difficulty accepting far-reaching conclusions that are not based on concrete data, logic, and a logical understanding of a problem.

The Midlife Transition: INTP and ISTP

Introverted Thinking Style: Precision—Define Your Terms

INTP

Nothing is more important than
original thought.

ISTP

If you don't talk straight, I won't
hear you.

Characteristics of INTPs and ISTPs

- Difficulties with relationships at work and at home
- Anger at a midlife process that they don't understand and which they find disruptive
- Risk taking
- Inability to know and express their feelings
- Demands for freedom

Particularly True for INTPs

Deep, slow searching for their true selves,
which demand acceptance

Particularly True for ISTPs

Discounting of and impatience with
processes that are not always
understood or valued

Relationship Issues

Other people (depending partially on their own type preferences) may

- Experience them as judgmental of others and the helping process
- Experience them as unaware of their feelings and embarrassed by emotion
- Experience them as resistant to anything they perceive may limit their freedom

Others should try to

- Understand their own needs and biases and be empathetic to the person's resistance to anything that they can't understand or explain
- Appear competent and unthreatened while avoiding too much structure and caretaking

INTP ISTP

<table>
<tr><td>

*Particularly with INTPs,
others should try to*

Affirm their cognitive preference and
need for recognition of their integrity
and precision

</td><td>

*Particularly with ISTPs,
others should try to*

Respect their need to address
a concrete problem, which
is almost always present

</td></tr>
</table>

Guidelines for Helping INTPs and ISTPs Through Midlife

Recognize and confirm the strengths of introverted thinkers—their logic, analysis, ability to describe what they know, and demand for accuracy and accountability

<table>
<tr><td>

*Particularly with INTPs,
others should try to confirm their*

Ability to participate in deep
introspective searching

</td><td>

*Particularly with ISTPs,
others should try to confirm their*

Ability to interact with the
everyday world and to take action

</td></tr>
</table>

Encourage balance to introverted thinkers (which will also help them develop their feeling skills) by

- Helping them recognize the limits of rationality
- Helping them see the benefit of appropriate vulnerability
- Encouraging them to come to know and express their feelings, particularly gratitude
- Encouraging them to be more accepting (and less judgmental) of themselves and others

<table>
<tr><td>

Particularly Helpful for INTPs

Point out the need for staying grounded
in what is "ordinary" and of acting as
well as contemplating

</td><td>

Particularly Helpful for ISTPs

Point out that there is more to
things than what is initially
apparent, a task that may require
patience and introspection

</td></tr>
</table>

Profile: ENTJ

Deandra was a well-known and highly respected lawyer in her community. If asked, most of her associates would describe her as being what most women want to be. She appeared bright, direct, and outgoing and seemed to live her life based on what she believed in. Today she began to talk to her sister.

"I've come here because I really want you to confront me about my family life," she told her. "You may not know it, but Jim has moved out again."

Tom, Deandra's 18-year-old son, had left home the year before, and now Jim, her husband, had left also. "I'm sorry," her sister responded.

"Well, he won't be back this time," Deandra continued. "I'm sorry it's turned out this way, but in some ways it's a relief. I was really tired of his complaining and the fact that he was doing nothing about his life. He never liked his work, but he wouldn't do anything about it. And he never helped me with Tom. Tom wouldn't do his school work—or anything else for that matter. I was the one who always had to get him back in school and patch up things he didn't follow through on. But I've come to you because I value Jim and Tom, and I really want to understand this. Some people think this mess is all my fault, which makes me angry, but I do want to know if any of this is my fault. You know me, and so I want you to tell me the truth. I want you to tell me if you think this is my fault."

Her sister felt uneasy and wasn't sure she liked the position Deandra was putting her in. Besides, she didn't know whose fault this situation was. She asked Deandra why they couldn't talk about this without having to figure out who should be blamed.

"Well, it must be someone's fault," Deandra responded, "or all this wouldn't have happened. I don't want my family to split apart, but sometimes I think people who have high standards are destined to live with conflict."

"Especially if they want to make others live by their high standards," her sister responded almost without thinking.

Deandra didn't seem to hear her. She continued to talk about the need to believe in something. "If you don't believe in anything, you just compromise," she said. "I feel I compromise whenever I know something and don't speak out, whenever I see ways that things could be better and don't do anything to make them better, and whenever I go along with things rather than try to change them. I feel as though I compromise when I let people do what they want instead of making them do what is best."

Deandra had strong convictions, and she didn't hesitate to convey them. This ability had served her well in the past and would probably continue to do so, but it also seemed to her sister to be the root of her problem. Deandra's sister realized how difficult it would be for Deandra not to feel she must keep family members "in line" and not want to change them when she was convinced it was in their best interest. She knew how difficult it would be for Deandra to help her husband and son be their own best selves rather than try to change them into her ideal. She didn't know what to say. She couldn't remember Deandra ever being unsure about anything. She asked Deandra if she had ever been uncertain.

Deandra, at first surprised, answered, "Yes, there was a time right after my first marriage broke up when I questioned everything. I wondered if the breakup were my fault and if I were strong enough to make a life of my own. I wondered about the meaning of life. I consulted with many people; I read self-improvement books; I explored other religions, even though I felt mine was the best. That period was horrible. But after everything I decided to go to law school, forget about the marriage and the questions, and make my own life. I'm glad that awful period of questioning is over."

Deandra's sister wondered what it was like when Deandra silenced the questions and the frustration and asked her how she felt when she decided to go to law school and forget about the marriage and the guilt.

"I felt it was the right thing to do," Deandra responded.

Then she asked if she thought there was "a right thing" she could do about Tom and Jim. Deandra said she didn't understand the question.

Deandra's sister felt uneasy and didn't know what else to do. Could her sister learn to explore without demanding an answer or outcome? Could she explore with her husband and son how each felt about the other and how each wanted to live? Could Deandra see the possible connection between her dislike of inadequacy and indecisiveness and the difficulties her family was experiencing? Deandra's sister suspected that Deandra used her quickness and ability to understand and conceptualize things to protect herself against feelings of inadequacy, lack of control, and incompleteness—feelings she couldn't accept in herself or others.

Turning to her sister, Deandra said, "I don't understand Jim and Tom. They know what they need to do, but they don't do it. I need to understand them. When will I?"

"Maybe you never will, and maybe you don't have to," her sister answered. Deandra did not understand.

Summary of Observations: ENTJ

- Deandra, like many ENTJs, appears articulate, competent, and strong.

- Deandra is easily annoyed by what she perceives as a lack of responsibility in others and is quick to assign blame to herself and others.

- Deandra feels a strong sense of responsibility for the behavior of others.

- Deandra "solved" her difficulties by using willpower and discipline.

- Deandra uses judgment to substitute for the expression of emotions.

- The missing parts of Deandra's personality—flexibility, vulnerability, and openness—are needed to complement and support her gifts of strength, power, and self-assuredness.

- Deandra's need for understanding may also be used as a defense mechanism to protect her from engaging in and experiencing limitations and inadequacy.

Analysis: ENTJ

Deandra's painful family situation may offer her an opportunity to grow, for she may meet forces she cannot change and cannot understand. If she can stay with her situation and not rationalize it away or try to "fix it" too quickly, she may learn something about the limitations of willpower, cognition, and power. She may also come to understand process as well as outcome, thereby gaining a more inclusive view, and becoming more approachable and content in the process.

Deandra must understand as much as she can and then apply her understanding to her actions. These are the gifts that she must honor at the same time that she acknowledges their limitations. Deandra's considerable skill in managing parts of her life must be honored, even as she becomes aware of her inability to manage some parts of it, particularly her personal relationships. She coped with the failure of her first marriage and the questioning that resulted from it by consulting authorities, reading, making external adjustments, and exercising willpower. This is typical of earlier stages in life, and it can allow for good accommodation and adjustment. At midlife, however, failure can offer an opportunity for more than adjustment; it can offer an opportunity for transformation. In Deandra's current situation lies the opportunity for her to feel how painful it can be to have relationships continually fail. She can learn about feelings of disorientation, lack of control, and the inadequacy of self-sufficiency. From her current difficulty she can learn that she needs help and that she can ask for it and receive it. She can learn about her limitations and come to realize that others may love her in spite of them.

As she begins to look inward as well as outward, her auxiliary introverted intuition and her introverted feeling, if she can access them, can lead her to a different territory. This inner terrain may feel foreign and uncomfortable to Deandra. To make friends with herself, she will need to slow down her frantic pace, calm her demands for closure and movement, and be more open to a nebulous, cloudy, noncognitive kind of understanding. To navigate her inner territory, she will need to spend time focusing on it by doing such things as taking solitary walks, exercising, meditating, writing, and talking about her ideas and feelings. She may need to simply keep a record of her feelings until she can recognize them more easily. This time may feel unproductive to her, for the inner world will not meet her time schedule. The information it presents will not be clear, logical, or rational. It may feel strange, bizarre, and untrustworthy to her. It won't fit into categories and may seem incomprehensible. But if she is strong enough to bear it, the connection of her outer and inner worlds may make her more open, approachable, and forgiving. And while this may be initially painful to her, it can lead her to happiness through a greater connection with others.

In typological terms, Deandra has a great asset to help her relate her inner and outer worlds. Her second function is introverted intuition, which is quite at home in the inner world, but which in her case has been poorly attended to. She has judged it (with her strong extraverted thinking) as bumbling, nonrational, confused, inadequate, and unuseful. Her extraverted thinking has obviously served well in helping her to understand and let go of a failed marriage and establish a healthy, productive career. Professionally, it has helped her establish a place in a society that highly values extraverted thinking. But it has also cost her in the development of its opposite—introverted feeling—and of her auxiliary function, introverted intuition.

Her introverted intuition and her even less developed or respected introverted feeling are her road map to the future. When she can approach her auxiliary introverted intuition, she may find that it can present her with many ways of perceiving and is quite comfortable with leaving options open. If she can attend to it, she may be relieved of some of the pressure she feels to make immediate judgments of options or to implement change quickly.

Her introverted intuition may help her to see that there can be many levels of truth and that truths that are sometimes learned from instinctive sources don't necessarily fit into categories, concepts, or generally formulated principles. This new way of thinking may help her realize that truths may not have to be explained or even understood. She may find herself being freed from the necessity of finding and enforcing objective "truth," and may instead recognize when she needs to act and when she needs to let things alone. She may grow to respond to people rather than attempt to mold or control them.

If she can also activate some of her sensing function, it, too, can take some pressure off her. With it she may be able to live with things as they are, as well as how they might be. She may be able to live for the moment and enjoy it without worrying about the future. Ordinariness—her own and that of others—may become more acceptable to her. With better development of her sensing function, she, like most intuitive thinkers, may be able to access her heart and body, as well as her mind for information.

Her introverted feeling, if she can accept it, will help her greatly in getting to know what is important to her. It may feel out of control and primitive, but it may also lead her to greater happiness as she comes to know what she values. It will be difficult for Deandra to honor this function, not only because it is her inferior function but also because it is the inferior function of her society and profession. She may find herself drawn to it, particularly the warm intimacy of its subjectivity, but she may also greatly fear it and its resistance to objective, general principles that apply fairly to everyone.

In fact, she may discover that fairness cannot always be generally defined. She may wonder how the feeling function can make decisions and may fear that if it does make decisions, they will be "fuzzy" ones that she can't defend. Yet she may feel greatly enriched by its gut-level assurance and its ability to declare that there are personal values that do not need to be explained or justified. If she can become comfortable with this type of subjectivity and its power, she may find that she is also capable of allowing others to hold their own personal values.

Deandra's midlife task requires that she come to understand the complexity of understanding what is true and right for others. She will feel less driven, less judgmental, less defensive and more connected, relaxed, accepting, and open when she can make connections with her inner subjective, personal, and ever-changing sources of data and can learn to live with mystery, vulnerability, and humility, all of which result from recognizing limitations and ordinariness.

Profile: ESTJ

Byron had just been told that he was being offered early retirement at age 55 and was to talk with his company's outplacement consultant. It was clear to the consultant that one of his roles was to ease the conscience of management, but he also knew that Byron could use someone to talk to. Even so, he wasn't looking forward to the meeting. Byron was a large, impressive, slightly intimidating man, who appeared in control of things.

"You know all about what's happened," he said to the consultant. "What can you do for me? Looks like I'll have to get my resumé up to date and get ready to hit the pavement," he said, answering his own question. "They brought you here, so how are you going to help me?"

Byron knew how to apply pressure, and he wanted to know what he could expect from the meeting. He wanted to confirm that the consultant was competent, and he wanted to know how long this process would take. Byron wanted to plot the territory. The consultant wanted Byron to talk about what had just happened to him.

"I got fired, that's what just happened," said Byron, seemingly annoyed to state the obvious.

"Yes," the consultant said, "but I really don't know all about the situation. I wish you would fill me in."

Byron wasn't eager to do this. He wondered what good it would do, but he complied and began to describe how he perceived his retirement offer.

"Last year, we were involved in a merger," he began. "In that process, I acquired a new boss who never appreciated my work. I know how to do my work; I've been doing it, and doing it well, for twenty-five years. Yet he always comes down here with all these ideas. He wants things done in all these new ways, and he expects me to do an about-face. He didn't even want to hear about how we do things around here. I've been loyal and have worked hard for this company for my entire working life. It isn't fair for him to come in here from the outside and tell me to change my ways. And he also gave me a bunch of new direct reports who don't carry their weight. If my people don't work, I let them go. But here are these new people who don't work and I'm told not to fire them. We have a lot of work to do. I've been working twelve to fourteen hour days for a year, and these people just don't produce. Why should I have to put up with them?"

He stopped talking. There was anger along with feelings of underappreciation, stress, and fear. What would a 55-year-old man who had worked twelve to fourteen hour days for twenty-five years do when he didn't work?

Byron was tired of talking about his job loss. He asked the consultant for direction. They discussed job hunting strategies, resumé reviews, and interviewing techniques. The consultant also asked Byron about his family, specifically about how they might take the news of his retirement, and if he might like to use this period of flux to examine other options.

"I'd like to explore with you what kind of life you live—or want to live— outside of your work," the consultant told Byron. "Are there things you haven't done that you may want to do now that your time will be freer? Do you think you might want to replace your job with one similar to it or with one entirely different? You'll probably need to explore your financial situation."

"My finances are in good shape," Byron said. "Maybe there isn't enough money to last forever, but my home mortgage is paid in full. The company also gave me a good retirement package—it relieves their guilt," he added, "but it may not be enough to last forever. I'm only 55."

The consultant then asked if Byron wanted to look for another job that would require him to work twelve or fourteen hours a day.

"Well, what else would I do?" Byron asked.

"Tell me what you would like to do," the consultant responded. Byron didn't know how to respond. "Tell me how you're feeling now," said the consultant, trying again.

Byron hesitated and then said, "I feel very tired."

"Then I guess what you want to do is rest," the consultant said.

Byron agreed, but thought he should plan to start looking for a job. He didn't think he should waste time. Byron felt strongly about not wasting time, but added, "If there were time I could do lots of things."

"What kind of things could you do?" he asked again.

If there were enough time, Byron thought, he could grow a garden, build furniture, do charitable volunteer work. Byron was surprised at how appealing the prospects were to him. He thought about his wife. His retirement could be very different for her. He wondered if they were ready for this.

Summary of Observations: ESTJ

- Byron appears direct, focused, and in control, and he needs to believe that the consultant is competent.

- Byron is impatient with therapy talk that he feels is useless.

- Byron expects and demands hard work of himself and of others. He is suspicious of innovation, especially by newcomers.

- With Byron, like many other ESTJs, it is helpful to begin with specifics and later try to expand options and widen focus.

- Byron's great need for security has led him to pay careful attention to practical matters.

- Byron finds it hard to assess his feelings, and his sensing function, particularly his body awareness, may help him with this.

- Byron realizes that both he and his wife will have adjustments to make, since they are both accustomed to him being a busy, self-sufficient provider.

Analysis: ESTJ

Byron's forced retirement throws him abruptly into a period of transition. In this period, his everyday objectives and his work, through which he largely defines himself, are taken away. This vacuum leaves him feeling out of control. He also feels angry at being unfairly treated, for he knows he worked hard and deserved better. His first reaction is to try to reestablish control quickly by returning to what he knows best—by getting a new job and putting his life structure back in order. Yet this very loss of life as he knows it and his inability to carry on in his customary way offers him an opportunity to explore other ways of working and living. He also has the opportunity to decide what really matters to him, not just to his employer.

Byron's natural tendency to size up situations and act on his findings needs to be honored. His immediate needs must be attended to. His tendency to size up things and take action will help him move ahead in his new life, but it can also protect him against any frustration and confusion, which, though unpleasant, may provide opportunities for new growth. His inability to get things back to normal quickly externally may give him the opportunity to look to himself. This freedom from structure, responsibility, and roles may allow him to explore his options and personal values, if he can cope with the ambiguity of "not knowing what to do."

In typological terms, it will be especially hard for Byron to value ambiguity and subjectivity. His extraverted thinking looks to general principles, laws, codes, and creeds to provide life guidance and expects them to be adhered to. Principles offer safety and assurance, and they offer clarity, which his sensing and thinking functions greatly value. Yet Byron finds that one strongly held general principle—that hard work and loyalty always get rewarded—has just crumbled. This makes him angry and shakes his sense of safety, order, and justice. It also causes him pain, for he feels undervalued. If he can access his introverted feeling, which he may be able to do by understanding the steps of grieving and recognizing how they relate to him, he may know that he is not only angry but also very hurt and afraid. He may also realize that he can confirm his own worth, as well as accept the judgment of external authorities. He may be surprised and delighted when he learns the sense of power that comes from inner authority, as opposed to external authority that is based on rules and roles.

It will be difficult for Byron to feel comfortable with his introverted feeling function. Like all introverted functions, it will take time to develop. If he wants to experience the benefits of introversion, he must slow down his pace and nurture his introversion, though not turn his life over to it. He may become frustrated because introverted feeling is not only slow but is also hard to name and define, and is almost impossible to control. He will fear it, for he believes it lacks efficiency and practicality. Introverted feeling's highly charged energy also seems dangerous to Byron because it almost feels as though it may wash him away. It will be best for him to approach his introverted feeling with care, which is how everyone should approach their undeveloped functions. He may discover in this undeveloped function that the vulnerability that it creates in him makes him more accessible to others. It may provide a new way for him to relate to his wife and to others. He may feel less sure and in control but may also feel more connected and interdependent.

His sensing function, particularly his introverted sensing, may be his guide to his feeling function. His well-developed sensing function might help him pay attention to his physical responses, and they may provide insight into his needs and values. For example, his feelings of physical weariness tell him he needs quiet and rest, though his extraverted thinking concludes that this is inappropriate for someone who "should be looking for a job." His sensing function, if he can quiet his dominant thinking function long enough to hear it, can help him focus on the moment, on the particular, and keep him away from abstraction. If he can free it from its demands for productivity, he may come to know the sensing gifts of simple enjoyment and of allowing things to just be, rather than trying to control them.

His intuition will also help him. It can provide him with options and possibilities—and enthusiasm. His intuition, as he develops it, with its tendency toward expansiveness, will break down boundaries that have limited the way he thinks about himself and his world. His forced retirement has broken his external boundaries, which were defined by roles, rules, and schedules. His intuition can break his internal boundaries and fill in the void with new ideas about himself and how he wants to work and live.

Byron's midlife task will require that he expand his sense of self to include more than what he does or produces. He will feel less tired, stressed, unappreciated and will feel more spontaneous, enthusiastic, and relaxed when he takes the time to explore his many options by consulting his wishes as well as his sense of responsibility and his need to be productive.

Typological Descriptions: ENTJ and ESTJ

ENTJ	*ESTJ*
Going as far as I can—and further	*Find the facts and move on*
Dominant extraverted thinking	Dominant extraverted thinking
Auxiliary introverted intuition	Auxiliary introverted sensing
Tertiary extraverted sensing	Tertiary extraverted intuition
Inferior introverted feeling	Inferior introverted feeling

For both ENTJs and ESTJs, dominant extraverted thinking is in charge. They focus their lives on resolving problems, reaching conclusions, and moving on. Experience tells them that their strategies will work. They look outward for information—reading books, talking with others, and seeking data from the external world. Sensors are most likely to be convinced by specific data and facts. Oriented primarily toward the practical, concrete, and nonpersonal world, they have little patience with lack of clarity and theory, which they often see as idle speculation, unless it is substantiated by what they consider to be sufficient, relevant data. For them, there are no hidden agendas and no messages between the lines. Since they need an inherent structure and order in their work environment, they will create one if it is not already present before proceeding with established routines, structures, and traditions. They prefer to have information presented with logical sense and order, which enables them to move more quickly toward a decision.

Both types, with their dominant thinking preference, have an almost instinctive tendency to solve problems. For ESTJs midlife may bring about an increased focus on looking at possibilities and options and learning not to reach closure too quickly. ENTJs may become increasingly grounded in the here-and-now, looking for more practical ways to solve problems. In midlife, they often become more comfortable with relinquishing some of their control needs when appropriate, encouraging the increased involvement of others in the decision-making process. In midlife, both types enjoy incorporating more of the SP characteristics—doing things just for the fun of it, not to become competent or to have control. Allowing the more spontaneous and free sides of their personalities to develop, they can become more in touch with their "playful child," enjoying the moment for what it is, not for what they can make of it or how they can structure it.

Developing their inferior feeling function often becomes the major midlife task for both types. Since the core of extraverted thinking is taking charge and being in control, introverted feeling may move them toward increased awareness of their own values. Ultimate questions such as, "What is my life really about?", "Does my life have any meaning?", Who can I trust?", and "What do I want to do with the rest of my life?" may become increasingly important to them. Awareness of their own inner values may change some of the ways they structure their lives. It can also provide them with an increased awareness of their emotions.

ENTJs

ENTJs need to do things their way and often resist taking instructions from others. Their deep sense of personal integrity necessitates their belief and honest commitment to the things they're involved in. They tend to see many approaches and facets to situations. They enjoy confrontation and exchanges of ideas, and thrive on lively verbal interchange. Like ESTJs, they set goals and priorities and then move toward closure.

Not prone to dwell on emotions, they may become increasingly moody or out of character. For some thinkers, therefore, integration of their inferior feeling function requires a conscious effort, that is, thinking about how to act in a feeling way. Getting in touch with inner feelings often relates to becoming connected with the physical reactions and learning to use them as clues to naming the feelings.

ESTJs

ESTJs tend to resist change unless they can understand the rationale behind the change and how it will affect them. They often worry about inconsequential issues before they even occur. At midlife, however, they may become more open to other possible options and new possibilities as long as they have sufficient time to reflect on them; however, they are more likely to oppose change if they think that tradition is being threatened. They prefer to recognize problems when they occur and move ahead toward quick action. They follow standard organization procedures and may have little tolerance for those they deem to be inefficient. At midlife, however, they often become increasingly aware of the need to express more frequent appreciation and praise, both in their professional and personal relationships.

The Midlife Transition: ENTJ and ESTJ

Extraverted Thinking Style: Keep On Keeping On

ENTJ

Pain is past tense.

ESTJ

If it ain't broke, don't fix it.

Characteristics of ENTJs and ESTJs

- Intense external trigger events (initiators) that break through "life as usual"
- Conflict in work and/or relationships and unresolved grief
- Feelings of being out-of-control, driven, tight, stressed, overworked, and resentful of disruption
- Quick pace
- The extraverted thinking attempt to manage the transition period (i.e., set goals and strategies and implement them)

Particularly True for ENTJs

Inability to live with limitations and high competence needs (fear of vulnerability) that can prohibit movement

Particularly True for ESTJs

Inability to see options and high security needs (fear of risks) that can prohibit movement

Relationship Issues

Other people (depending partially on their own type preferences) may

- Feel pressured and judged by them
- Sense their resistance to and great discomfort with lack of clarity and the slow, uncontrollable nature of the midlife transition

Others should try to

- Understand their own needs and biases and be empathetic to the person's resistance to introspection and emotions
- Appear confident, competent, active, and respectful of them

Particularly with ENTJs, others should	*Particularly with ESTJs, other should*
Encourage acceptance and an honoring of failed attempts	Offer alternatives and practical, concrete suggestions

Guidelines for Helping ENTJs and ESTJs Through Midlife

Recognize and confirm the strengths of extraverted thinkers—their commitment to order and principles and their willingness to bear responsibility and take action

Particularly with ENTJs, others should try to confirm their	*Particularly with ESTJs, others should try to confirm their*
Strengths of good conceptualization, verbal fluency, and political savvy	Strengths of focus, practicality, and diligence

Encourage balance to extraverted thinkers (which will also help them develop their feeling skills) by

- Emphasizing a respect for others' views

- Encouraging recognition of reality and trustworthiness of knowledge that is not cognitive (i.e., knowing by exploring feelings, hunches, experiences, body sensations, dreams, fantasies, etc.)

- Raising awareness of the limitations of sweeping statements of principle and the need for recognizing subjectivity and personal, individual differences

- Discouraging the tendency to take total responsibility to "fix" things or find an answer

- Encouraging the acceptance of ambiguity

- Encouraging recognition of the importance of process as well as product and of relationships as well as tasks

Particularly Helpful for ENTJs	*Particularly Helpful for ESTJs*
Encourage recognition of limitations and an attention to ordinariness	Encourage risk taking and expansion of boundaries

Part 3

Further Explorations on Type

Chapter 6

Gifts of the Spirit

*Spirituality is the courage to look within and trust.
What is seen and trusted appears to be a sense
of belonging, of wholeness, of connectedness,
and openness to the Infinite.*

C. G. Jung

For many, a more focused awareness of spirituality signals the ending of the midlife transition period and ushers in the period of reintegration. As we have seen, reintegration includes the integration of a personal, inner search, an enriching sense of relationship and connection with others, the identification of companions on the journey, and a deep sense of having a spiritual connection.

This is true for all types, but with the benefit that a knowledge of psychological type provides, we can begin to identify how spirituality relates to different types. What does "having a spiritual outlook," as Jung termed it, mean for an ESTJ as opposed to an INFP, for example?

In this chapter, we offer our findings in terms of how psychological type can influence the spiritual nature of the midlife experience. Men and women in midlife have shared with us glimpses of their spiritual experience during this central transition period, helping us to identify some common themes as well as typological differences.

Types Experience Spirituality Differently

The sensing and intuitive polarity presents one of the most significant contrasts in spiritual experiences. Sensing types often have difficulty describing their spirituality, although it is very real for them. Their spirituality emphasizes the depth significance of the *lived* life, as one sensor said, focusing on what they can do to live out their faith in the external world through their behavior in relationship to God, themselves, and others. Sensors tend to focus on specific interactions with individuals and groups in everyday life by asking themselves such things as, "Am I doing what I should be doing," and "Am I missing something?" Built on what is known, their spirituality is generally grounded in the present, focused on an acute awareness of the moment and the here-and-now. The "doing" self of sensors, especially in the case of extraverted sensors, is a form of prayer. For some sensors, especially SJs, having accepted traditional religious teachings, now is a time that they begin to question more, relying on their own experiences for increased insights and understanding. For them, spirituality is not focused so much on the mystical as it is on exploring reality-based data to determine what is concrete and applicable to their present environment. They ask themselves, "How does this connect with my own personal experience?" or "Is this true for my life?" When their search becomes less deliberate, they are increasingly able to listen for answers, even when they cannot formulate the questions.

In contrast, spirituality for intuitives provides an increasing awareness of the numinous as they make connections within themselves that seem to match their inner voices—the voice of the unconscious. They see new possibilities, new connections, a sense of hope and rebirth, and new paths of spiritual growth. Intuition helps them soar beyond the moment, allowing them to find links to new, exciting, and challenging dimensions of their beliefs. Fitting all the pieces together can be an ongoing and stimulating process, as they search for threads that can provide them with necessary connections. For intuitives, spiritual growth may emerge from paying increased attention to the reality of the present moment, being receptive to the spirituality of the here- and-now without trying to change it. With increased appreciation of the virtues of good health, they may be more aware and able to recognize physical symptoms that may signal disease, listening more carefully to the messages their bodies send them regarding their state of well-being.

Thinkers need to conceptualize and understand spirituality and then identify how it affects their lives. Their concept of spirituality influences the way they view the meaning of life and their place in the universe. Challenged and intrigued by the meaning and understanding of doctrine and its congruence with their lives, they often push against the limits of understanding, relying on objective truth articulated with conceptual clarity. At midlife, thinkers may come to know the limits of understanding and conceptual clarity and come to appreciate mystery and awe. At midlife, the feeling function of thinkers, with its emphasis on personal relationships and intimacy with a personal God, may be the pathway to a new dimension of spirituality.

For feelers, spirituality is a personal journey—a pathway toward growth and wholeness. Extraverted feelers often focus more on community, social consciousness, and connections with others, especially during the first half of life. Having always "been there" for others, at midlife they often express an increased desire to experience their own inner life in new ways. Introverted feelers talk about the need to reframe their lives by seeking answers to fit their own inner experience. They see their search for the "real me" as an inner journey to the spiritual. They tend to see spirituality as a gift—not something they do—and focus on developing an authentic relationship with God. All feelers need to tell their own stories and be heard and affirmed by others. Through telling their stories, their shared experiences help them affirm and validate their own stories through the commonalities they find and the understanding and personal affirmation they receive from others. As they begin to recognize similarities, identify patterns, and clarify their own experiences, they are increasingly able to move ahead.

Extraversion and introversion provide a different focus to this journey. For both extraverts and introverts, experiencing new dimensions of spirituality can enhance their deep, personal experiences at midlife. The

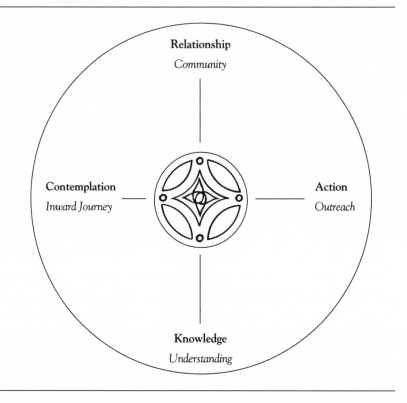

Shalem Model

Shalem model, shown above, is derived from a mandala used at the Shalem Institute in Washington, DC, and identifies four paths toward wholeness. Finding a comfortable balance between the dimensions of relationship/knowledge and action/contemplation can help each of us integrate our inner spiritual journeys with our outward expression of faith and beliefs. Jung (1965) recognized that "outward circumstances are no substitute for inner experience" (p. 5). At midlife, our spiritual task is to integrate whatever focus we have tended to neglect during the first half of life in order to find spiritual balance between these four paths. Extraverts may find meditation and spiritual reflection to be welcome additions to their active lives, while introverts may experience new energy from increased community service and involvement. The image of the Celtic cross in the center of the Shalem model reflects sacred time and the union of opposites. "Make it so time is a circle and not a line" is inscribed on the back of the original mandala from Ireland.

Meeting in groups of people whose types are alike helps some people share their spiritual journeys with others. However, even among people in these groups, we have found that there are both commonalities and significant differences between people's spiritual experiences. The following profiles describe the common dimensions of midlife as people of each of the sixteen types have described them. The descriptions are paired on the basis of their similar experiences.

ISFJs and ISTJs

For ISJs, spirituality focuses on the "depth significance of the lived life," the significance of the concrete reality of each day, or what meaning is real in everyday life. One ISJ group at a midlife workshop began their assignment by focusing on doing, having an "S" experience by going for a walk together. Through their actions, they chose to affirm their internal sensing world, relinquishing "shoulds," "oughts," and external expectations by focusing on what they most wanted to do, what was valuable to them at that moment. By building on what they received from the past and what they experience each day, ISJs evolve as they search. Questions such as, "Am I doing what I should be doing?" and "Am I missing something?", are common during the spiritual journey of ISJs. Simply talking about their experiences is not enough. Their focus needs to somehow relate to the meaning of what they do. Their spirituality is generally not mystical; it is very present, grounded in the here-and-now. Introverted sensors appreciate religious externals as symbols that point to an unseen world. During reintegration, they often feel a pull toward their inferior function—intuition—with all its benefits and difficulties. The symbolic world may unexpectedly show itself in the form of dreams and fantasies, providing them with new and powerful ways of tapping into their spiritual lives.

ISFJs

ISFJs tend to personalize their search for spirituality by asking, "Do I have the right to be my own person?" They may wonder if something is wrong with them, since they have often lived their lives through serving others. Achieving clarity by finding their own truth may enable some ISFJs to relax their reliance on the "shoulds" and "oughts" that have often guided their lives. They can then avoid being controlled by others' mandates and focus more on intentionally listening to their own inner voices. Affirming their own internal world can relieve some of the pressure to fill expected roles. While ISFJs like their lives to be in order and be prepared for whatever may happen, they may wonder at times whether the slow, measured process and its ensuing struggle are worth the risk. An effective process for discerning their own truth often involves telling their own stories and listening to the stories of others. During one particular midlife workshop, an SFJ group began to identify how Murray Stein's model of midlife related to them. Without much discussion, they immediately began to tell their own stories and listened to and supported one another. Focusing on Stein's model was less important to them than sharing their own experiences. Several group members mentioned the difficulty of finding congruency and reconciliation between what they believe and do now and what they learned from a traditional religious standpoint.

ISTJs

ISTJs talk about the need to validate their own experiences. "I was eager to grasp the meaning of my own story," said one ISTJ, "and when

I did, I was less afraid to be me." One ISTJ had begun to wonder whether he wanted to live the way he had been for the rest of his life. The question led him to realize that his life could be what he, and not anyone else, made it. Having lived the first half of his life primarily through his family, children, and work, he was now increasingly drawn toward examining new choices and options for himself. As ISTJs learn to accept what they can't explain logically, they are also increasingly willing to relinquish some control and trust the process with greater comfort. Recognizing that there may be several different and equally valid solutions, they also begin to trust that the answer will emerge. Aware of a continually strengthening spiritual base, they continue to search for specifics, even as they become increasingly comfortable with the general, or the big picture.

ESFJs and ESTJs

For ESJs, just talking about spirituality is not the answer. They often have difficulty finding the right words to express themselves, tending to focus instead on what they do and on external events and activities. The "spiritual" is often too abstract for them, though every now and then they catch a glimpse of it. Generally less interested in ultimate questions, they tend to focus more on behaviors, outcomes, goals, and priorities. For them, the spirituality of the "lived life" expresses itself through active membership and involvement in groups that offer them the chance to focus on their spirituality. Understanding what they believe and following the appropriate guidelines for living provide ESJs with a framework for living out their faith in the world. Although they often choose to stay within the organizational structure, at midlife they may begin to pay an increasing amount of attention to inner guidelines as they weigh against outer dictates. As they become more open to what they can't understand, they are more attracted to the mystery and symbolism of their chosen faith.

ESFJs

ESFJs focus on relationships, often aligning themselves with others by always being available to those who need them. By keeping busy in the outer world, their lives become very rich. They focus not so much on "Who am I?" but on "How do I fit into relationships and make significant contributions to the community?" ESFJs ask, "What can I do for you and/or the organization?", focusing on the present situation, accepting it as it is, and tending not to bring up anything from the past. Intellectualizing is often fatiguing for them. They prefer to live out their spirituality by reaching out to those in need, enabling them to ease the personal pain of others in a concrete way. Although they may be accused by other types of avoiding the issue, talking is not the answer for ESFJs, but doing what is necessary and then moving on is. Structure becomes a strategy for moving ahead. At midlife, identifying and naming their own experiences can provide ESFJs with more inner definition for understanding their individual journeys. Their pain focuses around separation from community when their personal journeys lead them away from collective ideas.

ESTJs

Though ESTJs continue to focus on external events, they slowly begin to move from an external to an increasingly internal self-definition. This internal sense is often based on an integration of their own personal value system, as they begin to incorporate new dimensions of their feeling function. "I don't think I ever thought before of what *I* wanted," said one ESTJ, referring to his internal values. At midlife, however, as ESTJs exchange some of their "shoulds" for "wants," they find themselves moving toward increased inner awareness of who they are. They begin to see the "many sides" of truth. This does not negate, however, the importance of the institutions they are a part of. One ESTJ found that his spirituality was reflected in his membership in many organizations and through his efforts to meet the needs of others.

ENTPs and ENTJs

ENTs also tend to concentrate on the external world. The NT temperament wants to understand, and tends toward global, not personal, spirituality. At midlife, more focus on their personal inner world and increased recognition of the limits of rational thought may help them develop spiritually.

ENTPs

ENTPs often ask, "What *is* the inner life?", as they focus on the external realm of action, possibilities, and options. They want to understand, not control the situation, and just let go and see what happens. Their desire to keep moving often diverts them and others from focusing on their own internal world, thus enabling them to protect themselves by keeping others off balance. Frequently seeking inner, spiritual answers through others, ENTPs may be drawn to outer systems through such things as astrology, talk shows, and the experiences of others. They often avoid the difficult task of getting in touch with their own emotions. They reject "emotionalism" in others and especially in themselves, often masking any intense, inner reactions with an outer facade of calm. At midlife, they may learn to slow down their pace of living to become more contemplative, listening more to their inner voices as well as to feedback from their environment. Increased awareness of their own emotional and physical sensations may help them integrate their sensing and feeling dimensions.

ENTJs

ENTJs tend to experience an increased connection with the spiritual part of their lives in midlife more easily than ENTPs. As their focus often shifts to an internal center, they ask, "What do I really want?", "What is my life all about?", "Does it have any meaning?", and "Who can I trust?" Increasingly drawn to their inner lives, they often become less interested in controlling the world and become more responsive to others, as well as to their own needs. "Getting on with life" is an important goal of ENTJs during this process. Impatient for the process to reach closure and being true to type, they seek to devise a working plan, a blueprint, follow it through, and then move on.

INTJs and INTPs

INTs, above all, seek authenticity and integrity in their spiritual focus through a sense of increasing congruency between their inner and outer lives—between who they are and what they do. They try to find the missing pieces by identifying where they fit in best. Maintaining a sense of personal integrity is a priority for both INTJs and INTPs. Both types tend to assign blame to themselves and others, reflecting their tendency to set high expectations. For both, relaxing their dependence on rationality as the primary way to spiritual life may help them become increasingly open to unexplored paths through art, nature, and dreams. They may also experience greater congruence through awareness of their inner values and discovery of new ways to integrate them with their spiritual lives.

INTJs

For INTJs, the spiritual journey is intensely personal and often hard to discuss with others. They tend to avoid groups in which others talk about their personal experiences or beliefs on a superficial level. As one INTJ group reported, "Our discussion was so deep and personal, we couldn't put anything down on the newsprint." This particular group of people, which spent a weekend together, was able to talk deeply with each other, but not with those who were not a part of their experience. INTJs tend to have difficulty articulating their emotions, which, like a land mine, are often susceptible to exploding if they are stepped on. For them, spirituality is not only a personal quest; it is also finding answers to the questions, "How does this fit together?" and "What is the logical pattern here?"

Their need for inner and outer congruency may lead them to ask who is responsible, to question their own competence, and to assign blame. As one INTJ explained, "If I don't fit into the grand plan, it must be my fault." Seeing the patterns and the grand design is important to INTJs. Questioning often brings them to focus on what they want to spend their remaining time doing and being. Like ENTJs, they are eager to set strategies and then move on. Maintaining one's personal integrity, always an important issue, becomes even more critical for INTJs at midlife.

INTPs

INTPs feel as though they have been seeking all along, almost waiting for the world to catch up with them and accept them. Having always been drawn to a sense of what is "spiritual," INTPs are pulled further along toward finding a purpose in life during midlife, discovering the missing parts, and letting go of attempts to "fit in," focusing more instead on being who they are. Less concerned with control, they are more interested in being of service to others while continuing to maintain their own integrity. For them, life is too short to sell out to conventional success goals. Since they don't assume that outside organizations or other people necessarily have answers for them, they are not concerned with the "shoulds" and "oughts" of individuals and systems. They tend to choose personal fulfillment and integrity over worldly success—a systemic harmony that is congruent with their sense of self. Unlike INTJs, they want to let go of responsibility and focus more on just being. For them, the process becomes more important than setting strategies and moving on.

ENFJs and ENFPs

ENFs speak of constantly focusing on the process of *becoming,* of self-actualizing. Their developing relationship with their spirituality, themselves, and others during midlife often leads them to "do justice," as they become increasingly conscious of social issues in their local communities and throughout the world. Their search for meaning often comes through their community and relationships and through a sense experience of oneness with others. ENFs live and breathe relationships. In midlife, they often become more reflective and less accepting of given answers, seeking a core of authenticity from within themselves.

ENFJs

As ENFJs become less accepting of answers from the external world, they become increasingly affirming of their own value and worth. The search becomes less deliberate and focused as they try to be more open to oneness and wholeness, by asking fewer questions and being less dogmatic and sure. As one ENFJ said, "I learned that life was happening even as I planned it. Maybe it's okay not to have answers." As she increasingly recognized that the search process itself had its own value, she began to experience increased openness to new pathways. "I am learning to let go of the ideas I felt I should have accomplished in the past and increasingly look forward to future possibilities." Like ESFJs, ENFJs gradually move from the external messages that reflect external "shoulds" and "oughts" to a greater focus on listening to their own inner core.

ENFPs

ENFPs thrive in the external world. Many speak of reassessing their lives, seeking increased authenticity, wanting to be true to their own personal values, not just accepting what they have been taught or following guidelines established by others. One ENFP described this process as "getting more in touch with that energy source that comes from deep within and is intensely private." Some ENFPs ask whether they can truly live with an independent enough spirit that they have less need of specific relationships to live creatively and joyfully. As a type that thrives on relationships, ENFPs may struggle intensely with this issue. A common theme focuses on spiritual connectedness, trusting the process of "being on the path and learning to trust the spirit to show me the gifts within this unease." For them, expectant waiting and reflection, along with increasing discipline and focus, become useful tools for the spiritual journey.

INFJs and INFPs

For INFs, spirituality is a gift, not something they do. Increasing self-awareness often leads them to a deeper relationship with their spirituality. The pathway toward growth and individuation is an "inner journey to the spiritual," a mystical trusting of the spirit within. They focus on the search for their real selves, learning to trust the answers that come from within. One INFP described this process as a "cosmic understanding" that relationships are all that matter.

INFJs

For INFJs, struggling with ultimate questions of spiritual and personal meaning is likely to be an integral and constant part of their lives. They have always asked "Why?" in their search for purpose in life and their desire to understand it. They often struggle between coping with and accepting their differences and seeking a sense of connectedness with others and the external world. Life for them is an ongoing process—a journey, a validation of themselves through the recognition of their own worth. Their intensity is reflected in their desire for increased depth as their introverted intuition spirals to deeper and deeper levels of meaning. Learning that their inner intensity may alienate and frustrate others, they often engage their internal censor in "testing the waters" to see what is safe to share with others. As dominant intuitives, they often express a great desire to understand by reframing life in a way that makes sense to them.

INFPs

INFPs are also overwhelmed by the intensity of "emotions in turmoil." For many, the focus for change comes from inner spiritual experiences, their own inner journeys. Seemingly always aware of their differences and having always struggled with ultimate questions and personal meanings, they continue the journey throughout midlife. However, they now yearn to become increasingly content just "to be," no longer feeling the need to prove themselves. Appreciation of their dominant feeling function by learning to validate their own personal value systems helps them become more centered. As one INFP expressed it, "a deep sense of spiritual reality helps me believe in life and trust that it is a process of continued enrichment." Increased self-acceptance, often triggered by a knowledge of the MBTI, enables INFPs to be more accepting of who they really are. Finding new ways to relate to people, while still retaining their sense of integrity with the inner core of their being, can become a challenging and exciting part of the spiritual journeys of INFPs.

ESFPs and ESTPs

ESPs want to be involved in the process of spirituality, to experience it for themselves. "We aren't searching for the meaning of life, we are life," said one ESFP. They prefer to tell their own stories rather than attempt to relate to and understand the stories of others, which may often be quite different from their own. The telling often enables them to clarify and understand their own experiences. They tend to have a flair for the dramatic, wanting to see their personal experiences from several different perspectives.

ESFPs

ESFPs express the need for companions in their spiritual journeys, recognizing that it may become too uncomfortable or dangerous to travel alone. For them, spirituality is not identified as a path or journey toward something in the distant future but as an appreciation of the present moment, a part of the life process. At midlife, they often become increasingly aware of their own inner experiences and feel less need to rely on answers from others. Slowing down the pace of life, therefore, may help them look within themselves to validate their own concrete experiences without weighing them against what they have been taught or have learned from others. Gifted with people, they bring a sense of contagious enthusiasm to their spirituality, as they reach out to help others in specific, concrete ways.

ESTPs

ESTPs recognize the reality of paradox and want to be actively involved in the changing environment and the relationships around them. Their "bottom line spirituality," as one ESTP put it, helps them find something that works for them. At midlife, with both feet grounded in the reality of the present moment, they can then become more open to recognizing other inner, spiritual dimensions available to them.

ISTPs and ISFPs

ISPs often find their spirituality both in the world of nature and in their relationships. One ISP spoke of the "meditative nature of sitting in a duck blind." Another recalled the sense of awe she experienced as she photographed a mountain covered with snow. The moment when things are "more than they seem"—beyond concrete reality—can be a spiritual moment for ISPs.

ISTPs

ISTPs talk about focusing on concrete realities in a logical, practical way. As their feeling function surfaces more fully at midlife, they talk about wanting to be understood and accepted for who they are without being "swallowed up by relationships." Recognizing their need to maintain a deep, inner sense of integrity within both personal and professional relationships, they often seek a partnership that enables them to connect with another person on a deep level. Especially at midlife, they appreciate people who will help them "touch" the deep emotions within themselves in an atmosphere of safety and care.

ISFPs

ISFPs need a practical approach to spirituality that emphasizes sensitive, feeling relationships. A deep spiritual connection with others helps them validate their own worth. They need to feel accepted just as they are, to be valued without having to struggle or prove their worth to others. With increasing comfort, their deep sense of caring can lead them to champion causes that support their inner values in increasingly extraverted ways by reaching out to others in need.

Examples from our workshops and counseling sessions continue to validate central themes of spirituality that apply to all types, although specific expressions may differ. During midlife, our continuing development tends to center on our desire to become more whole and to honor our own inner reality and uniqueness. Continuing development at midlife calls us to shift our focus from ego—and its tendency to accommodate others—to self, which can help us recognize and validate our own inner reality. Jung believed that telling our own stories as an integral part of the process can help us identify and reclaim our own personal stories at increasingly deeper levels. Listening to stories from different people, we are reminded that although an increased focus on identifying one's own spiritual path is a common theme for everyone, the specific directions and expressions of those paths may vary.

Jung (1933) understood spirituality to be at the core of the midlife experience. "We moderns are faced with the necessity of rediscovering the life of the spirit. We must experience it anew for ourselves," he said (p. 122). Jung's comment continues to be applicable to us more than a half century after he said it. Midlife is a time for "growing a soul," a time for paying increased attention to our deepest, inner spiritual center. Jung understood spirituality and integration of the self to be the lifelong goal of our psyche. Early in his career, he raised two great questions that he later answered throughout his life: "What is the secret of the human personality?" and "What is my own personal myth and the myth of time?" (van der Post, 1975, p. 270). We, too, in our various paths toward individuation, might ask ourselves the same two questions framed in our own language.

Chapter 7

Gifts of Type

This chapter presents a summary and overview of the typology described in this book and developed by Jung and Myers as a way to understand personality. These charts do not capture the whole of type but give a representative picture of the most common characteristics. For further explorations, consult any of the works listed on the References and Resources pages at the back of this book.

Characteristics of Dominant Functions

Each type has a dominant function, one that is more accessible and available to consciousness. For example, extraverted thinking is the dominant function of ENTJs and ESTJs; introverted feeling is the dominant function of INFPs and ISFPs. The dominant function will generally be used in one's preferred direction for energy flow, either introverted or extraverted.

Extraverted Sensing
ESFP and ESTP

Are stimulated by external sensory data

Have an acute awareness of their environment

Are expansive

Rely on observable facts

Attend to the present moment

Live life to the fullest

Are gifted problem solvers

Focus on the "possible dream"

See life as an exciting experience

Introverted Sensing
ISFJ and ISTJ

Pay selective attention to outer stimuli

Have precise, rich, internal impressions

Have a highly focused need for limits

Have an internal categorization of data

Are attuned to physical sensations

Process data sequentially

Have a realistic respect for facts

Perceive things subjectively

Need to see the relevance of details

Extraverted Intuition
ENFP and ENTP

See new options and possibilities

Express themselves easily

Are energized by expanding interests

Have a constant sense of optimism

Are committed to their visions

Are stimulated by new directions

Have a broad range of interests

Have an expansive vision of life

Focus on future visions

Introverted Intuition
INFJ and INTJ

Recognize symbolic patterns

Search for archetypal gestalts

Focus on new connections

Seek new dimensions for understanding

Are attuned to unconscious images

Trust processes to unfold

Feel an unexplainable nagging sense

May have difficulty translating their visions

Live in an intense inner world

Extraverted Thinking
ENTJ and ESTJ

Focus on objective analysis

Are interested in broad concepts

Value decisiveness and closure

Live by definitive rules and laws

Seek workable solutions

Identify what needs to be done

Organize their external environment

Move quickly from data to closure

State ideas clearly

Are well-ordered, ultimate planners

Introverted Thinking
INTP and ISTP

Are absorbed with inner thoughts and ideas

Are influenced by subjective data

Seek clarity of information

Need to categorize and prioritize

Attend to inner principles

May have difficulty communicating their ideas

Adapt to processes

Seek to understand general concepts

Base logical ideas on new visions

Order their lives through inner structure

Extraverted Feeling
ENFJ and ESFJ

Focus on relationships

Seek harmony with others

Are friendly, sympathetic, and helpful

Are attuned to the social needs of others

Are conscientious of their responsibilities

Enjoy responding to others

May sacrifice themselves for others

Need external validation

Are loyal to friends and organizations

Introverted Feeling
INFP and ISFP

Live by deep, internal values

Rarely articulate their values to others

Seek realization of values in the world

Show warmth and loyalty to a select few

Have a quiet influence over others; set norms

Need inner harmony with self

Are loyal to whatever they value most

Have a low need to control others

Seek coherence at home and at work

Common Midlife Tasks By Type

Each type typically has certain attributes that need to be honored and certain ones that need to be integrated at midlife. The following summaries, though incomplete, identify characteristic patterns people continue to describe.

ISTJ

Things to Honor. Clear focus; rich internal impressions; a willingness to work and take a stand on things; groundedness; and solid and deliberate pace, particularly where change is involved. Also honor the need for a competent guide who can offer specific, concrete steps and tasks that "make sense" to ISTJs

Things to Encourage. To know the cost of taking on too much responsibility; to break from routine ways of behaving and being; to contemplate the meaning of life experiences; to expand ways of knowing beyond the cognitive and concrete; to be enthusiastic and optimistic; to concentrate on relationships and relaxation as well as task and production; to see the paradox of things; to let things happen as well as make things happen; and avoid compulsiveness

ISFJ

Things to Honor. Clear focus; rich internal impressions; willingness to work and take suggestions from others; groundedness; and a solid deliberate pace, particularly where change is involved. Also honor the need for a supportive, caring guide who can offer suggestions, support, and enthusiasm

Things to Encourage. To know the cost of taking too much responsibility; to break from routine ways of behaving and being; to contemplate the meaning of life experiences; to give up on and let go of obsolete ideas, relationships, and work; to be enthusiastic and optimistic; to expand beyond the personal and the immediate; to enthusiastically believe in and care for oneself; to see the paradox of things; to let things happen as well as make things happen; and avoid compulsiveness

ISTP

Things to Honor. Real, down-to-earth approach to life; flexibility; an internal sense of order; ability to analyze and name precisely and succinctly what is happening and to act when it seems appropriate. Also honor the need for a guide who appears competent to help the client deal with the specific, intermediate issues presented and to hold one accountable

Things to Encourage. To know that there is more than is immediately apparent; to be aware of one's emotions and to relate to others; to recognize personal pain; to be appropriately vulnerable; to tell one's personal stories; to know that growth may be important for its own sake; and to recognize the value of connection through relationships

ISFP

Things to Honor. Deep value orientation; tendency to care deeply for people, causes, and ideas, especially those in their immediate circle and the disadvantaged; the ability to adapt to the real world; gentleness, kindness, and idealism; flexibility and the ability to act when it seems appropriate. Also honor the need for a guide who can provide encouragement and support, and hold one accountable

Things to Encourage. To know that there is more than is immediately apparent; to confront and not discount or run away from things that are troublesome; to tell one's personal story in order to find direction from inner values and to express these values and personal warmth in the outer world; to weigh the consequences of one's actions; and to have faith in oneself and to become more assertive and open

ESTP

Things to Honor. Ability to observe real-life phenomena and recognize it for what it is; ability to demand competency; tendency to enjoy life; ability to make difficult decisions and act quickly, spontaneously, and decisively; and the need to take an active role in the process of counseling. Also honor the need for a guide who can competently challenge and push beyond the limits of what is concrete and rational, and who can also confront one and hold one accountable

Things to Encourage. To slow down, contemplate life experiences, and entertain the idea that there might be more than what is immediately obvious; to entertain the possibility of an inner imaginative life as well as an outer, pragmatic, action-oriented one; to accept the reality of paradox and ambiguity; to realize that pain must be faced; to see that the past and future, as well as the present, must be considered; to value the importance of relationships as well as tasks; to take small, deliberate, thoughtful steps and to avoid overloading on details

ESFP

Things to Honor. Ability to enjoy life and to observe real-life phenomena and recognize it for what it is; ability to relate to others with warmth and spontaneity and to act quickly and decisively. Also honor the need for a guide who can competently challenge and weigh the consequences of actions and who can hold one accountable

Things to Encourage. To slow down, contemplate the deeper meaning of life experiences, and entertain the idea that there might be more than what is immediately obvious; to know that there can be an inner imaginative life as well as an outer action-oriented one and that one's inner values can provide guidance as well as a sense of control over one's life; to accept ambiguity and paradox as things that are real; to realize that pain must be faced; to know that the past and future, as well as the present, must be considered; to take small, deliberate steps, find role models, avoid overloading on details, and be true to oneself, even if it means being separated from and misunderstood by one's community

ESTJ

Things to Honor. Diligence; a willingness to take responsibility; breadth of involvement; analytical ability; an ability to organize and create order; and a grounded, practical approach. Also honor the need for a guide who appears competent, confident, directed toward immediate concerns, and who challenges others in a respectful way

Things to Encourage. To slow down decision making in order to entertain other options (even ambiguous ones); to access inner, personal values as well as expected outcomes when involved in decision making; to reflect on and tell one's personal story; to dream, imagine, and take new risks; to abandon an overreliance on self-sufficiency and personal responsibility and to be appropriately open; to pay attention to relationships as well as tasks; to realize one's limitations; to become aware of one's emotions, particularly negative ones like sadness and grief; to show positive feelings toward others and to play as well as work

ESFJ

Things to Honor. Ability to relate to others with warmth and empathy; diligence and discipline; action orientation; willingness to take responsibility for things; breadth of involvement; and grounded and practical approach. Also honor the need for a guide who can actively offer specific suggestions, support, and encouragement as well as challenge them to see things in new ways

Things to Encourage. To learn to attend to one's own needs even if it means not pleasing others or doing things for them; to tell one's personal story and reflect on it; to know that one can come to trust one's inner values as well as outer responses for guidance; to learn to confront others and be assertive; to come to accept unpleasantness and negative emotions such as rage and betrayal; to slow down life's pace; to play as well as work; and to know that there are many possible ways of doing things

INFJ

Things to Honor. Vision; intensity; depth; ability to see patterns; relational gifts; individuality; sense of responsibility and determination. Also honor the need for a guide who can listen and offer affirmation and encouragement

Things to Encourage. To validate nudgings and urgings received from the unconscious; to develop personal power; to make one's inner vision real in the outer world; to develop confidence; to come to recognize one's body signals, which can provide important data; to learn to confront others when necessary; to relinquish some of the tendency to please others; and to modify perfectionistic tendencies when they become personally harmful

INTJ

Things to Honor. Vision; intensity; depth; ability to see patterns and to conceptualize things; clear, focused analytical abilities; sense of responsibility and organization; sense of integrity; and ability to make and stand by difficult decisions. Also honor the need for a guide who can confidently be receptive to the person's inner, authentic truth

Things to Encourage. To validate nudgings and urgings from the unconscious, as well as rational thought, in order to discover one's own inner, personal truth; to give up blame of oneself and others; to come to recognize one's body signals, which can provide important data; to entertain the possibility of mystery or the possibility of things that cannot be known; to learn about one's limitations and weaknesses; and to come to know and appreciate one's own emotions and express them to others with trust and warmth

INFP

Things to Honor. Deeply held values; intensity; a willingness to risk being heard in struggle for personal growth; the need to tell one's personal story; deep, personal introspection; ability to see many possibilities; ability to be adaptable and to live with process. Also honor the need for a guide who can listen patiently, provide support, and help one focus on and become grounded in reality

Things to Encourage. Necessity of living in an imperfect world; to learn to let values give basis for choice making; to learn to weigh the consequences of one's actions; to follow one's own unique rhythm; to entertain the idea of both objective and subjective truth; to release some inner tension in appropriate ways; to entertain the possibility of making appropriate compromises when necessary; to express inner values and warmth; and to focus on and implement things

INTP

Things to Honor. Depth and precision of thought process; originality; ability to analyze and name things; need for accuracy and competence; adaptability and ability to live in process. Also honor the need for a competent guide who can respect, challenge, and hold one accountable

Things to Encourage. To learn to connect with others and the world while retaining individual integrity; to communicate things that haven't yet reached total internal clarity; to come to experience things rather than to "know about" them; to come to know one's emotional climate, especially negative emotions, such as sadness and grief, and to share these with others; to become more accepting and less blaming of oneself and others; to show warm feelings to others; and to be appropriately vulnerable and to accept one's weaknesses, limitations, and ordinariness

ENFP

Things to Honor. Enthusiasm; vision; breadth; ability to see possibilities and connections; adaptability; flexibility; and warmth. Also honor the need for a guide who can affirm people and their ideas as well as assist them with focus and reality testing

Things to Encourage. To slow down and develop an awareness of inner values that can focus activity and offer a sense of personal control of life rather than a sense of reacting to whatever offers stimulation and/or pleases others; to make ideas and visions "real"; to weigh consequences of actions in the moment; to become aware of body signals, which can provide important data; to focus on and stay in the present; to take small, deliberate actions; and to learn about ordinariness and personal and societal limitations

ENTP

Things to Honor. Enthusiasm; vision; breadth; ability to see possibilities and connections; ability to conceptualize and communicate new concepts. Also honor the need for a guide who can live with process and can challenge the person to see beyond cerebral understanding and to make ideas and concepts real

Things to Encourage. To slow down and develop an inner awareness that can enable one to focus on what is personally important rather than be diverted by too many possibilities; to be careful and thorough; to ground things and make them real; to get in touch with body signals that can provide important data; to stay in the present and take small deliberate action steps; and to learn about ordinariness and personal limitations

ENFJ

Things to Honor. Ability to relate to others with warmth and empathy; need for harmony and fear of disharmony; discipline and diligence; responsibility; need to tell personal stories and desire for personal growth; quick pace; and grasp of possibilities. Also honor the need for a guide who can support and interact with the person

Things to Encourage. To pay attention to inner, personal values as well as collective and interpersonal ones; to prioritize values and be assertive about adhering to them; to see that one's own growth and the growth of other people may be related; to deal with negative emotions such as rage and betrayal; to integrate identity and intimacy needs; to focus on and live in the present with its limitations and ordinariness

ENTJ

Things to Honor. Devotion to rational process; ability to organize and manage; sense of order and fairness; responsibility; ability to make difficult decisions and to act on them; and ability to see possibilities and to conceptualize things. Also honor the need for a competent, active guide who can respectfully challenge defenses against ambiguity and vulnerability

Things to Encourage. To entertain many definitions of truth; to discover and express one's emotions, including sadness and grief; to accept one's limitations and weaknesses as well as those in others; to trust ways other than cognition as a means of knowing; to slow down and seek inner as well as outer direction; to accept the reality of ambiguity and paradox; to be appropriately vulnerable; to accept the viewpoints of others (even when they are not understood); to express positive, warm feelings toward others; to honor process as well as product or solution; to honor relationships as well as tasks; and to play

Common Midlife Tasks By Preference

For people who are unsure of their complete type code but who have some clear preferences, it might be helpful to summarize a key midlife task by letter preferences. There are many more tasks, but these seem critical for midlife development.

Extraversion	*Introversion*
To discover the inner, personal meaning of external stimuli	To connect one's inner, subjective vision to external, objective reality

Sensing

Extraverted Sensing

To slow down, reflect on, and come to know the meaning of life experiences

Introverted Sensing

To expand one's horizons and make necessary changes with hope and enthusiasm

Intuition

Extraverted Intuition

To learn to limit, focus, and ground visions in order to make them real

Introverted Intuition

To learn to explore and validate one's inner visions in order to communicate them confidently to others

Thinking

Extraverted Thinking

To realize the limitations of cognitive understanding and to entertain the possibility of the existence of multiple truths

Introverted Thinking

To know one's emotions and to express them to others

Feeling

Extraverted Feeling

To pay attention to one's own inner values as well as the desires of others

Introverted Feeling

To validate one's own inner values and express them in the external world with confidence and warmth

Judging

To relax the need for answers and certain outcomes, with its tendency toward excessive responsibility and judgment of oneself and others

Perceiving

To be responsible and accountable for a diligent and faithful follow-through to processes that are undertaken

Chapter 8

The Inferior Function
and the Shadow at Midlife

Integrating the Inferior Function

At midlife, most of us continue or begin the difficult process of integrating more of our inferior function, which tends to be the weakest part of our personality, since much of it remains unconscious and is the rejected and often neglected part of our personality. Jung (1971) said that "the inferior function always puts us at a disadvantage, because we cannot direct it, but rather are its victims" (p. 540). Although we have used our inferior function in various ways throughout our lives, at midlife it is likely to assume a more prominent role. When we focus on meeting the expectations of individuals, groups, and institutions during the first half of life, we often neglect our inferior function. Therefore, it often remains immature, primitive, inexperienced, and outside of our conscious control. Most of us have learned to use this function effectively at particular times to support our dominant function—during carefree or playful experiences or when we felt confident in our actions—all of which are positive ways to integrate the inferior function.

More often, however, and especially when we are under stress, the inferior function can tyrannize us with its seeming independence and our inability to control it. At the slightest criticism or provocation, we may suddenly and unexpectedly react in the most uncharacteristic and hostile ways. Our inferior function is most likely to appear when we are feeling stressed, depressed, unsure of ourselves, and/or are physically or emotionally exhausted. It primarily asserts itself through *projection*, the attribution of various aspects of our own characteristics, attitudes, or desires to others. Whenever we talk about another person, we tend to project our own needs, desires, or weaknesses onto them through either positive or negative projections. Positive projections may offer us glimpses of potential growth and development that we have not yet recognized in ourselves. Although negative projections occur throughout our lives, they become increasingly common during midlife, when we seem to have less control over our lives. What we dislike but can't acknowledge in ourselves, we see all too clearly in others. At the same time, we attack certain characteristics in others without recognizing the presence of them in ourselves. At such moments, we often exhibit a sense of sensitivity that signals caution to others who might attempt to communicate or interact with us. When others learn to read these "caution" signs, they may avoid becoming drawn into painful and nonproductive conversations. Challenging someone in the grip of their inferior may only exacerbate the degree of negative intensity.

The inferior function may be identified by the following characteristics:

- Touchiness and tyrannical behavior
- Impersonal/collective responses
- Excessive slowness in responding to others
- Unavailability to rational feedback
- Immature, childish, or infantile behavior
- An unwillingness to listen to reason

- Sudden charge of energy
- Primitive/archaic expressions
- The use of emotionally loaded statements
- Out-of-character behavior
- Inability to listen to criticism

Characteristics of Inferior Functions

Each type has an inferior function (e.g., extraverted sensing is the inferior function of introverted intuition). The inferior function offers particular challenges. Some of the negative manifestations of the inferior function are listed for each type. The inferior function also offers opportunity because although it cannot be fully developed or integrated, it can serve as the conduit of unconscious material that offers new energy and exhilaration for our midlife journeys.

INFJ and INTJ *(when inferior extraverted sensing* *is operating)*	*ENFP and ENTP* *(when inferior introverted sensing* *is operating)*
Are closed to alternative possibilities	Are obsessed with physical symptoms
Are obsessed with detail and sorting	Become fixated with details
Are immobilized by external data	Can allow one fact to multiply into a disaster
Can become stubborn and compulsive	
Use facts to prove incompetence	Internalize others' negative judgments
Become compulsively busy	Push themselves physically to the point of exhaustion
Focus on gloom and doom	
Are unaware of their own inner physical signals	Are unaware of their outer environment
	Buy items they don't want or need
	Focus on selective facts

ISFJ and ISTJ
(when inferior extraverted intuition is operating)

Imagine only the worst scenarios

Have difficulty verbalizing distress

Get the job done—no matter what

Are down on themselves, have difficulty discussing things

Dismiss imagination as unreal

View alternative possibilities as unrealistic and improbable

Superstitions not backed up by data

Become overwhelmed with possibilities

ESFP and ESTP
(when inferior introverted intuition is operating)

See only dark, foreboding possibilities

Underrate themselves and their abilities

Become paralyzed by their inability to act

Consider external data to be irrelevant

Become cut off from others

Become depressed and can find no way out

Can have a sense of hopelessness

Can become stuck in lose-lose situations

INFP and ISFP
(when inferior extraverted thinking is operating)

Have an excessive need for control

Overintellectualize things

Allow their emotions to erupt inappropriately

Are often unable to defend their positions

Withdraw from relationships

Make impersonal, rigid judgments

Use logic to berate themselves with "If only" statements

May become sarcastic and hostile

May lash out at others and attack them

Critically focus on "being right"

ENFJ and ESFJ
(when inferior introverted thinking is operating)

Can be extremely insensitive

Appear cold, uncaring, and hostile

Attack others when their "logic" is challenged

Have difficulty articulating their experiences

Critique themselves and others harshly

Seek the "truth" from "experts"

Become defensive and retreat

Make inappropriate statements

Try to justify past actions

Become immobilized

INTP and ISTP (*when inferior extraverted feeling* *is operating*)	ENTJ and ESTJ (*when inferior introverted feeling* *is operating*)
Make devastating emotional attacks	May withdraw from others
Can be hypersensitive to perceived personal rejection	Are intolerant of their own and others' errors
Focus on inappropriate data to support conclusions	Are unaware of their own emotional needs
May use verbal jabs to lash out at others	Question their own abilities
	Have little control over their emotions
Can become inappropriately sentimental	May appear out of control to others
	Experience a sense of inner despair
Work hard to control their emotions	Rarely express their feelings
	Rigidly protect their own values

The inferior is not all negative, however, since it can serve as a bridge to our less conscious, symbolic world and help us make connections to unexamined and undeveloped parts of ourselves. Learning to "play" with our inferior at midlife can bring about a renewal of life for us by incorporating new and exciting dimensions of living. A variety of playful expressions of our own inferior functions may enable many of us to experience a renewal of life through a "childlike" exhilaration and sense of freedom.

The Shadow and Midlife

Because the inferior function is closest to our unconscious, it is also the primary channel for the appearance of the archetype of the shadow. Our shadow includes those unconscious, often negative, parts of ourselves that we have forgotten, have not yet developed, or repressed when they failed to fit our image of ourselves. Getting in touch with our shadow selves increases our awareness and motivates us to shift from ego to self, the central core of our being, and the process of reintegration. The shadow, in both its personal and collective form, can make itself known at any time in life, although it seems to become increasingly pervasive at midlife. During the period of liminality, our personal shadow, which contains some of the least acceptable qualities of ourselves, can more easily break through our beleaguered defenses. Robert Bly (1988) metaphorically describes the shadow as "the invisible bag we drag behind us" (p. 18). This "bag" contains parts of our personality, both positive and negative, that we hide from our own view and the view of others, choosing not to integrate them into our conscious personalities. When we are very young, says Bly, we have what he calls "a 360-degree personality." But somewhere early in life, we become aware that our parents, teachers, and/or peers don't like certain parts of our personality, so we stuff the parts that have been deemed unacceptable into our bag and then "spend the rest of our lives trying to get them out again."

We may reckon with our shadow in several ways by:

- Trying to get rid of it, either through repression (turning inward) or projection ("throwing it onto others")

- Acting it out or blaming others, assuming no responsibility for our own actions

- Recognizing our liabilities and learning to forgive ourselves

- Bearing the consequences of its expression and learning from them

- Integrating its assets and insights through increased acceptance of its presence in our lives

- Refusing to recognize and face it

The act of "making friends with our shadow," as William A. Miller (1981) describes it, is one of our most difficult and important tasks at midlife. We tend to wear off the rough edges of the qualities we expose to others through our ego, thus increasing our awareness, development, and acceptance of those qualities. Just as the ego is influenced by our type preferences, the shadow emerges most commonly through our nonpreferences—the paths of least resistance—our tertiary and inferior functions, the functions over which we have the least control. When qualities we repress or hide become a part of our unconscious, they tend to remain primitive and underdeveloped, erupting unexpectedly when they are exposed to specific triggers.

The positive sides of our shadow often include our creative potential and the areas of growth we may see mirrored in the lives of individuals we greatly admire. Midlife presents us with the opportunity to integrate those qualities into our own lives, not by trying to become like those we most admire, but by developing our unique potential.

When we make judgments of others, we tend to project onto them our own negative shadow, the inferior side of our personality that we often neglect in favor of our more developed dominant and auxiliary functions. Those discarded parts of ourselves that we are unable to integrate into our own lives often become the "hooks" through which we judge similar characteristics in others—and unconsciously—our own negative qualities. Often frightened by our unacceptable qualities, we seek absolution through criticizing others with similar qualities.

Judith Viorst (1986), in her book *Necessary Losses*, relates the story of a Holy Man in an ancient Kingdom, a story that reflects the integration of the shadow:

> There was once, in an ancient kingdom, a most famous holy man, renowned for his generous heart and his many good deeds. And the ruler of that kingdom, who esteemed the holy man, commissioned a great artist to paint his portrait. At a ceremonial banquet the artist presented the king with the painting, but when, with a flourish of trumpets, it was unveiled, the king was shocked to see that the face on the painting—the holy man's face—was brutish and cruel and morally depraved.
>
> "This is an outrage!" thundered the king, ready to have the hapless artist's head. "No, sire," the holy man said. "The portrait is true." And then he explained: "Before you stands the picture of the man I have struggled all my life not to become." (p. 179)

The holy man was able to recognize and own his shadow side to an extent that others rarely received his negative projections or were even aware of those characteristics. As we become aware of and develop our own personalities, we, too, can come to forgive ourselves, appreciate and value others, and have less need to project our own weaknesses onto them.

~~~~~~

Chapter 9

Expanding Dimensions
of Development at Midlife

Jung's original book on personality types published in 1923 was called *Psychological Type—The Pathway to Individuation*, thus identifying the development of personality as central to the individuation process. Grounded in our unconscious, type provides a lens or filter through which all other elements of psychological growth can occur. This lifelong process of typological development helps us gain greater control and expanding expertise with our abilities to perceive the world and judge our perceptions.

Jung identified one's personality by the primary orientation of a person's dominant function, that is, extraverted sensing, introverted thinking, and so on. Psychological type, therefore, provides a lens through which we can each identify our own path toward individuation and wholeness by outlining a likely pattern of development for each of the sixteen types identified by the MBTI personality inventory. Jung's image of type as a compass helps us to understand which preferences we tend to orient to the external world and which we tend to orient to our internal world. The mandala images that Jung used as symbols of the individuation process reflect the self.

During accommodation, both extraverts and introverts tend to inter-act with the outer environment with their primary extraverted function, generally the dominant function for extraverts and the auxiliary for introverts. With increased usage, situational fine-tuning, and affirmation from others, this function, which often receives the most attention, is likely to become our most dependable, reliable, and valued one. For extraverts, the dominant generally assumes this role. As Myers recog-nized, however, since the inner dominant function of introverts often receives less recognition and validation, their extraverted auxiliary—their primary means of interaction with the external world—often assumes the leading role during the first half of life. The concept of *introverted complexity*, as identified by Otto Kroeger (Kroeger & Thuesen, 1988), identifies the many ways introverts are often encouraged by the external world to focus on their auxiliary preference during accommoda-tion. For many introverts, midlife is therefore a time for increased recognition, development, validation, and trust of their inner dominant function. As they learn to extravert their dominant more frequently and with greater ease, introverts often feel increasingly comfortable, compe-tent, and in control of their lives.

John Beebe, a prominent Jungian analyst and author, expands our understanding of development through his image of a developmental mandala that identifies a vertical axis as our "spine" and a horizontal axis as our "arms," as the two mandalas in the figure on the next page (one for extraverts and one for introverts) illustrate. He divides the sixteen types into two categories—those with *rational* spines (thinking/feeling) and those with *nonrational* spines (sensing/intuition) and suggests that per-sonal interactions with those who have "spines" that are opposite our own may be fraught with heightened misunderstanding, especially when we are tense and under pressure. In addition, those who use their primary functions on the same spine—either rational or irrational, but in opposite directions, as the figure illustrates—may also experience confusion, uncertainty, and frustration in their attempts to communicate with and understand one another. For Beebe (1992), these opposites reflect one's shadow typology.

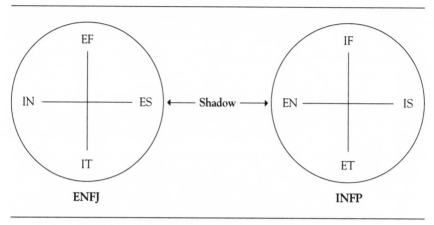

The Developmental Mandala

Our midlife data indicates that extraverts tend to focus on their spine—the dominant/inferior axis—during accommodation, developing and using their extraverted dominant with increasing skill and ease. During accommodation, however, introverts report that they are more likely to focus on their arms—the auxiliary/tertiary axis. As we have indicated before, the primary function we extravert during the first half of life, dominant for extraverts and auxiliary for introverts, generally tends to receive the most attention and often, therefore, becomes our most dependable and reliable function.

Like Harold Grant (1983) in *From Image to Likeness*, Beebe identifies alternating attitudes for our likely developmental patterns. In their models, our dominant and tertiary functions will generally be used in our preferred attitude—either extraverted or introverted—and our auxiliary and inferior functions will be used in the opposite attitude. In general, our data tend to support this developmental pattern. At midlife, as we continue to circle around the self, we become more intentional about seeking to integrate whatever parts of ourselves we neglected during accommodation. Jung's original model of development, symbolized in the image of a mandala, presents a holistic, developmental framework for all types, one that can help us identify and understand our own patterns.

Examples and stories from others have helped us clarify more about the role of the inferior function at midlife. Used primarily in the opposite direction from our dominant function (internalized for extraverts and externalized for introverts), we are often aware of the general discomfort and stress it may cause. Using our inferior function is like writing with our nonpreferred hand. We often feel awkward and clumsy, unsure of ourselves, and aware of the tension that surrounds our uncertain attempts to use them. As we have continued to explore our own experiences and have recognized patterns from listening to others, however, we are beginning to understand how our own inferiors, when used in the opposite direction to our dominant, can increasingly become a resource of great energy and exhilaration. Our "playful child" may often become activated, providing us with new sources of excitement into midlife and beyond.

For example, during accommodation, extraverted thinkers (with inferior introverted feeling) often become more aware of what is most important to them by identifying their own inner values, considering them as increasingly important and appropriate for making decisions. This awareness may also help them recognize the need to listen more closely to what others value, seeing this information as necessary for making decisions that affect others. They often seem more awkward and may have greater difficulty with extraverted feeling, however, which when integrated can help them become increasingly conscious of the need to express and demonstrate their appreciation of and caring for others with increased frequency, especially with those closest to them. This expression, in whatever form it takes, often requires conscious effort on their part by understanding the different ways in which others want to be appreciated, taking sufficient time to determine what they want to say and how they want to say it, and learning to express themselves appropriately.

Some extraverts tend to focus more on their inner auxiliary and their dominant in the opposite direction than expected during accommodation. Many ENFPs, for example, often extravert their feeling function, focusing on reaching out and caring for others. They tend to fulfill their own need to be loved and nourished by interacting with others in the same way through their warm, caring persona and their positive energy and enthusiasm. Keeping busy can become an excuse for ignoring their own inner pain and emptiness. "I've spent so much of my time caring for others...now who will care for me?", they often ask themselves at midlife. By intentionally learning to clarify their values, prioritizing which are most important, and caring for themselves as much as for others, they may feel increasingly centered, eager to reach out again as they experience a more appropriate balance between the extraverted and introverted dimensions of their "feeling." Like extraverted feelers (ESFJs and ENFJs) at midlife, they may retreat from continually responding to others' needs to claim some time, space, and direction for their own lives.

Introverted feelers, with inferior extraverted thinking, often become increasingly adept at expressing the logical ideas and rationale that support their deep-seated values in ways that convince others to support them. Their introverted thinking, however, is directed neither to "objective facts nor to general ideas" (Jung, 1971, p. 343). When entangled with inner thinking, they may judge individuals, organizations, and the world around them with sweeping generalizations that can often have a dark, cynical edge. When the shadow emerges through their introverted thinking function, they can become most uncharitable toward others, unable to recognize the good in anything or anybody, including themselves. When used in the same attitude as our dominant, therefore, our inferior may be even more closely connected to our deep unconscious— that dark, shadowy part of ourselves over which we have the least amount of control.

We can each learn to discern our own developmental sequence, discovering our patterns and identifying any missing parts of ourselves by looking back to reflect on our past experiences. Midlife calls us to recognize and become increasingly centered on our dominant/inferior "spine," the core axis of our personality. This is the hero and heroine's journey, centered around our dominant preference and lined up with our typological spine. As we continue to circle around our center, we can discover other dimensions of our development, identifying which functions (and in what directions) we have already integrated and which can continue to lead us into new, expanding dimensions of personal growth and understanding.

At midlife, both extraverts and introverts at midlife need to pay increased attention to their own inner work, becoming more centered on their "spine," the ego/self axis that connects with the deepest part of our being. This rich, spiritual center can guide our personal individuation journeys as we move toward fulfillment of our maximum potential as unique men and women, truly reflecting our individual gifts that continue to bring richness, relationship, and meaning to our lives.

Chapter 10

Using the Mandala to Explore the Midlife Journey

Mandalas provide an appropriate symbol for identifying different dimensions of type development, especially at midlife. As integrating symbols of the self and psychic wholeness, they represent the union of opposites, the process Jung called individuation. The type mandala can help us identify the polarities and the process of their integration in our lives during the second half of life. As we have seen, the task of individuation is to incorporate all the preferences as much as possible so that they are available and can be used appropriately. The pattern of development, as noted before, can be heavily influenced by both internal and external factors. Individuals on their own midlife journeys must discern their own patterns and recognize the importance of moving toward wholeness at midlife by incorporating to some degree of comfort each of the four functions and the attitudes of extraversion and introversion.

Jung identified the mandala as the central image of individuation, an integrating symbol of the self. It represents the union of opposites through the lifelong process of development. During accommodation, the mandala can help us clarify our own patterns of development by identifying which functions we have learned to trust and use most naturally and effectively.

Having been shaped by external messages from individuals, organizations, and culture, we often become most skilled at using those functions that are in our type code. At midlife, we continue to circle around the center, our image of self, integrating dimensions of type we tend to neglect during accommodation, such as:

- our mental functions used in nonpreferred directions (extraversion and introversion)

- increased validation of our inferior function and a recognition of its gifts

- movement from our accommodating self toward our "true" self

- integration of mental, emotional, physical, and spiritual energy

- increasing comfort and use of all functions as appropriate, recognizing that those in our type code will continue to provide us with our typological foundation

We can best learn how to use our nonpreferences when we are comfortable, free from stress, competent, and in control of our lives. Those who demonstrate competent use of these functions can provide us with appropriate models. Our goal should not be to "become" the opposite type, but to move toward increased integration of some attributes of the functions that are not in our type code. As we become more comfortable with our identity at midlife, we can enjoy the new energy that results from increasingly effective and appropriate use of all our functions in both introverted and extraverted directions.

The mandala can be used as a tool to demonstrate your path of type development and individuation. A blank mandala is included on p. 240 for this purpose. An example is also reproduced to show how one individual's path is charted on the mandala.

To chart your path of development and individuation on the mandala, first answer the following questions:

- Which functions and attitudes came more naturally to you during the first half of life? How did you use them?

- What function or functions did you use the most during the period of accommodation?

- Did your preferences fit environmental expectations, or did you often feel out of step?

- In what ways did you accommodate to others and your environment as a child?

- In what ways did you resist accommodation?

Now chart your own path of type development using the blank mandala provided to indicate which preferences you have integrated. After you have filled in your own type mandala, answer the following questions:

- Which preferences are you currently working on integrating? In what ways?

- Which preferences still need to be integrated more fully as part of your individuation process?

- In what specific ways can you be more intentional about incorporating other functions or the same functions in different attitudes?

- How will this integration help you continue to develop?

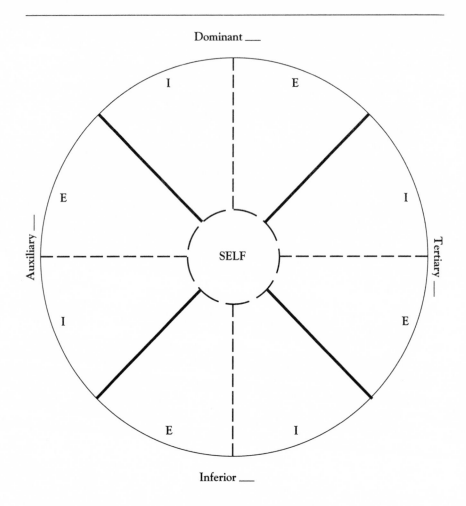

Dominant ___

Auxiliary ___

SELF

Tertiary ___

Inferior ___

Directions:
Label your dominant, auxiliary, tertiary, and inferior functions.
Describe briefly how you use each preference in extraverted or introverted directions.
Circle the letters of the preferences you have developed well and trust.
Draw arrows to indicate which preferences you are currently still working on integrating.

Name _____ Type _____ Date _____

Type Mandala

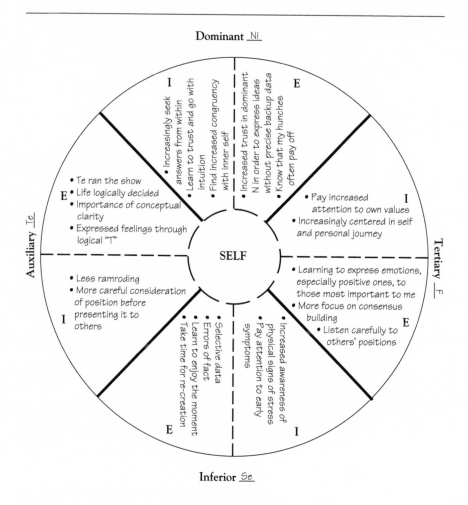

Dominant Ni

Auxiliary Te

Tertiary F

SELF

I
- Increasingly seek answers from within
- Learn to trust and go with intuition
- Find increased congruency with inner self

E
- Increased trust in dominant N in order to express ideas without precise backup data
- Know that my hunches often pay off

E
- Te ran the show
- Life logically decided
- Importance of conceptual clarity
- Expressed feelings through logical "T"

I
- Pay increased attention to own values
- Increasingly centered in self and personal journey

I
- Less ramroding
- More careful consideration of position before presenting it to others

E
- Learning to express emotions, especially positive ones, to those most important to me
- More focus on consensus building
- Listen carefully to others' positions

E
- Selective data
- Errors of fact
- Learn to enjoy the moment
- Take time for re-creation

I
- Increased awareness of physical signs of stress
- Pay attention to early symptoms

Inferior Se

Directions:

Label your dominant, auxiliary, tertiary, and inferior functions.

Describe briefly how you use each preference in extraverted or introverted directions.

Circle the letters of the preferences you have developed well and trust.

Draw arrows to indicate which preferences you are currently still working on integrating.

Name ___Mark___ Type ___INTJ___ Date ___5/23/93___

Example Type Mandala: INTJ

241

Acknowledgments

A book such as this cannot be written without the contributions of many people. We would like to express our gratitude to all those who have shared their experiences and personal stories with us in classes and workshops and through questionnaires and interviews. These people have helped us realize the value of making theory come alive. In a real sense, they are this book.

We would also like to offer a special thanks to Katharine D. Myers, who originally provided the inspiration and vision for this book as well as designed and presented the first midlife program centered around Jung's theory of lifelong development through the framework of the *Myers-Briggs Type Indicator®* personality inventory. For her wisdom and support, we are grateful.

Finally, we would like to thank the generous and knowledgeable people who read parts of our material and provided us with feedback, as well as Sheila Barrows and Martha Mabey, who read our manuscripts, and Paula and Larry Stein, Greg Walsh, B. J. Ware, Pat Gannaway, Jeannie Schlesinger, and Lin Koch, who assisted us with our typing and computers.

References

Beebe, J. *Integrity in Depth*. College Station, TX: Texas A & M University Press, 1992.

Bly, R. *A Little Book on the Human Shadow*. San Francisco: Harper & Row, 1988.

Browsword, A. W. *It Takes All Types*. Baytree Publications, 1987.

De Laszlo, V. S. *The Basic Writings of C. G. Jung*. New York: Modern Library, 1959.

Grant, H. *From Image to Likeness*. New York: Paulist Press, 1983.

Hall, C., and V. A. Nordby. *A Primer of Jungian Psychology*. New York: New American Library, 1973.

James, W. *Varieties of Religious Experience*. New York: Random House, 1961.

Jung, C. G. *Modern Man in Search of a Soul*. New York: Harcourt Brace Jovanovich, 1933.

Jung, C. G. *Memories, Dreams and Reflections*, edited by Aniela Jaffe. New York: Vintage Books, 1958.

Jung, C. G. *The Undiscovered Self*. Boston: Little, Brown, 1958.

Jung, C. G., ed. *Man and His Symbols*. New York: J. G. Ferguson Publishing, 1964.

Jung, C. G. *Psychological Types*. Princeton, NJ: Princeton University Press, 1971.

Kirton, M. *Kirton Adaptation Innovation Inventory Manual* (2nd ed.). Hatfield, UK: Occupational Research Centre, 1987.

Kroeger, O., and J. Thuesen. *Type Talk*. New York: Dell, 1988.

Levinson, D. et al. *The Season of a Man's Life*. New York: Ballantine Books, 1979.

Miller, W. A. *Make Friends With Your Shadow*. Minneapolis: Augsburg Publishing House, 1981.

Myers, I. with Myers, P. *Gifts Differing*. Palo Alto, CA: Consulting Psychologists Press, 1980, 1990.

Progoff, I. *The Well and the Cathedral*. New York: Dialogue House, 1977.

Stein, M. *In Midlife: A Jungian Perspective*. Dallas: Spring Publications, 1977.

Storm, H. *Seven Arrows*. New York: Ballantine Books, 1972.

van der Post, L. *Jung and the Story of Our Time*. New York: Vintage Books, 1975.

Viorst, J. *Necessary Losses*. New York: Ballantine Books, 1986.

Wall, S. "A Great Undying Spirit: Portraits of Native American Elders." *New Age Journal*, September/October 1989, 56.

Resources

Brewi, J., and A. Brennan. *Midlife: Psychological and Spiritual Perspectives*. New York: Crossroad, 1982.

Brewi, J., and A. Brennan. *Mid-Life Directions: Praying and Playing Sources of New Dynamism*. New York: Paulist Press, 1985.

Brewi, J., and A. Brennan. *Celebrate Mid-Life*. New York: Crossroad, 1988.

Bridges, W. *Transitions: Making Sense of Life's Changes*. Reading, MA: Addison-Wesley, 1985.

Campbell, J. *An Open Life*. Burdett, NY: Larson Publications, 1988.

Campbell, J., ed. *The Portable Jung*. New York: Penguin Books, 1985.

Chinen, A. B. *Once Upon a Midlife*. Los Angeles: Jeremy P. Tarcher, 1992.

Edinger, E. F. *Ego and Archetype*. New York: Penguin Books, 1972.

Frankl, V. *Man's Search for Meaning*. New York: Penguin Books, 1959.

Hirsh, S., and J. Kummerow. *LifeTypes*. New York: Warner Books, 1989.

Kopp, S. *If You Meet the Buddha on the Road, Kill Him!* New York: Bantam Books, 1972.

Loomis, M. E. *Dancing the Wheel of Psychological Types*. Wilmette, IL: Chiron Publications, 1991.

Miller, W. A. *Discovering and Fulfilling Your Underdeveloped Self*. San Francisco: Harper & Row, 1989.

Morrison, A., R. White, and E. Van Velsor. *Breaking the Glass Ceiling*. Redding, ME: Addison-Wesley, 1987.

O'Collins, G. *The Second Journey*. New York: Paulist Press, 1978.

Palmer, P. *The Active Life: A Spirituality of Work, Creativity and Caring*. San Francisco: Harper & Row, 1990.

Pearson, C. *Awakening the Heroes Within*. San Francisco: Harper-Collins, 1991.

Sheehy, G. *Passages: Predictable Crises of Adult Life*. New York: Bantam Books, 1977.

Sheehy, G. *Pathfinders*. New York: Bantam Books, 1982.

Sheehy, G. *The Silent Passage: Menopause*. New York: Random House, 1991.

Singer, J. *Boundaries of the Soul: The Practice of Jung's Psychology*. New York: Doubleday, 1972.

Spoto, A. *Jung's Typology in Perspective*. Boston: Sigo, 1989.

Tannen, D. *You Just Don't Understand*. New York: Ballantine Books, 1990.

Von Franz, M. L., and J. Hillman. *Lectures on Jung's Typology*. Dallas: Spring Publications, 1979.

Zweig, C., and J. Abrams. *Meeting the Shadow*. Los Angeles: Jeremy P. Tarcher, 1991.

Index